Maggy Van Eijk

REMEMBER
THiS WhEN YOU'RE

SaD

Published by Lagom
An imprint of Bonnier Books UK
3.08, The Plaza,
535 Kings Road,
Chelsea Harbour,
London, SW10 0SZ

www.bonnierbooks.co.uk

Hardback – 978-1-911600-73-2
Paperback – 978-1-911600-87-9
Ebook – 978-1-911600-74-9

A CIP catalogue of this book is available from the British Library.

Designed by Envy Design
Printed and bound by Clays Ltd, Elcograf S.p.A.

1 3 5 7 9 10 8 6 4 2

Copyright © Maggy van Eijk, 2018
Illustrations by © Flo B. Perry

First published by Lagom in 2018
First published in paperback by Lagom in 2018

For Annie and Sandy

Maggy Van Eijk

Originally from the Netherlands, Maggy moved to London to complete her MA in Writing for Stage and Broadcast Media at the Royal Central School of Speech and Drama. She spent a few years freelancing and selling Häagen-Dazs in West End theatres until she became the Social Media Editor for BuzzFeed. She now works as a Social Manager for BBC Three. Maggy has been writing about mental health for five years, and helped the BBC launch their 1 in 4 campaign during their mental health season. Maggy is based in London, and you can connect with her on Twitter @Maggyvaneijk.

––––––––––––

'This book made me feel less alone in a single page. It's reassuring, warm, hilarious, and without a doubt will help countless other people feel less alone as well, which is the best thing any book about mental health can do' –

Megan Crabbe (@bodyposipanda),
author of *Body Positive Power*

CONTENTS

The World Around You

BEFORE WE BEGIN

'Is this a good idea?'
'Is this a good idea?'
'Are we sure this is a good idea?'

This is the conversation I have with myself the most, sometimes out loud in the futile hope someone out there will reply. I said it when I told my doctor about my anxiety; I said it when I swallowed my first dose of Citalopram; I said it when I took myself to A&E; and I said it when I was thinking about writing this book.

Is it a good idea to write about something I'm still very much in the middle of? It feels like writing about war when I'm still on the battlefield or reporting on an earthquake when shockwaves are tearing down houses around me.

Deep down I know that writing this book *is* a good idea because it's what's helping me continue on. I have a Quality Street tin of mental health conditions that sometimes decide to get together and make a joint appearance. One condition at a time is relatively manageable but when they all flare up at once it feels like I'm walking around with my head on fire. Only, no one can see the blaze. Apart from the scars that run up and down my arms like train tracks, everything looks calm. Business as usual.

I hope that by writing out my story, by turning my brain inside out and making the invisible visible, I can help someone in a similar position; someone who feels they're stuck in the trenches and there's no way out. What I've learnt so far is that no matter how shit your situation is, there is an escape route and every time you climb out you'll be more equipped to deal with the next falling down. This book aims to remind people of that, and myself too.

Ultimately, your mental illness lies to you. It'll tell you that everything is wrong and that you have no future. It'll tell you that you should be ashamed and that you're a nuisance and you don't deserve to get help. The world in which depression and anxiety reign supreme is extremely lonely and I wanted to write this book to reach out and say: 'Hey there, you're not alone, I'm right there with you.'

Having said that, everyone's mind is unique and, whilst our background and diagnoses might sound similar, my story can't encompass your entire experience. In fact, diagnosis can be a strange thing. I was told I had unipolar depression at the age of seventeen, then a doctor came along and added bipolar to the mix in my early twenties, another one went back to the original conclusion and finally, aged twenty-seven, I was told I have borderline personality disorder. Each time I received a new diagnosis I assumed I'd step out of my GP's office and my entire life would change, but it never did. Instead my mental health remained the same tough slog of a thing I have to push through to move forward.

This book isn't specifically about my borderline personality disorder but it might touch on symptoms of that condition. I'll also touch on depression, anxiety, self-harm and self-esteem whilst moving through my body: the head, the skin, the gut, the heart and the world around me. I'll talk about the moments we all have when we're stressed, angry, sad, or all three. When you're plummeting into a sinkhole. When you feel so lost you could do with a map that tells you where you are and where you're most likely going to be tomorrow.

Depression is in no way equal to 'sadness' but I am sad an awful lot. So I've also filled this book with little everyday reminders to pull myself out of my brain ditch. There are notes and anecdotes plastered all over my walls,

3

my phone, my notebook, my mirror and the back of my hand, and I've put them all together on paper in a way I hope you'll find useful. Some of these reminders are set up as lists. I love lists. They impose a sense of organisation onto a lot of the chaos that whizzes around in my head. I make daily to-do lists. I make them for work. I make them for when I get home. I make bigger picture lists: week goals, month goals, year goals. I also have lists for things to reward myself with: tattoos, books, films, playlists.

The most important aspect of lists for me is the fact that they are a direct link to the future, even if it's as immediate as what I'm going to be doing in the next half an hour. Lists tell me I need to hang on. They tell me not to give up just yet which is why I'm using them so often in this book. Hopefully they'll have the same effect on you too.

Whilst I hope to offer you the best advice I can, it's important to remember that there is no blueprint to experiencing a mental health problem. There's no one-size-fits-all solution either. Personally, I've found reading about other experiences to be enlightening and comforting so I hope this book can achieve that for you. If anything you read makes you feel stressed out or uncomfortable make sure you speak out and ask for help.

Now let's begin.

The Head

REMEMBER THiS WhEN THE WORLD WON't StOP SPiNNING

PANIC AT THE DISCO

I'm twenty years old standing at the top of Row Mead and I'm about to die. Amy Winehouse has appeared on Glastonbury's Pyramid Stage. She weaves a halo over Worthy Farm with her booming voice and erratic yet hypnotising movements. She's singing 'Back to Black' and I'm trying to drink in the words that I've come to know so well, but there's a problem – something awful is happening to me. I'm pretty sure I'm dying.

In between 'Cupid' and 'Back to Black' my legs had turned to jelly, my stomach somersaulted, acidic dread had climbed up my throat and, as I fell towards the muddy grass, I hoped someone would tell my family I loved them, because this was it. At the very least I was losing my mind; at the worst my life was about to end.

I opened my eyes and realised I was somehow not quite dead yet. My boyfriend P. lifted me up and carried me to the medical tent, assuring me along the way that yes I was still breathing. The nurse handed me a plastic cup of water and suggested I go lie down in my tent and lay off the MDMA. I wanted to tell her I'd never done drugs in my whole life, but something told me she wouldn't believe me. I was ushered back outside where Amy was still playing somewhere in the distance.

I hoped my weird dizzy spell was a fluke but we had to cut our Glastonbury trip short: whether I was standing in a crowd of Kings of Leon fans or waiting for falafel in front of a food truck I kept experiencing that surge of feeling, like my-life-is-ending-right-this-second. I was constantly sprinting back to our tent to cry and hyperventilate into my sleeping bag.

When I left Glastonbury and returned to my student life in Bristol I convinced myself that whatever happened at the festival was the result of dehydration or perhaps a dodgy sandwich. But then a couple of days later it hit me again on the bus, then again in the student union bar and again in lectures and one-on-one tutorials. In the moments in between attacks I didn't feel right either. I felt disconnected from everything around me like my head was stuck in a snow globe. I barged into the doctors convinced I had diabetes, a brain tumour, chronic fatigue, an iron deficiency, vertigo, meningitis, Ebola, Alice in Wonderland syndrome (yes this is a thing), migraines, IBS and meningitis again. I did test after test but I was constantly told that I was in perfect health. During my fifty-sixth trip to the doctor a new GP saw me and asked how often I drank alcohol: 'Barely ever.' And how often I did drugs: 'Never.' He put his pen down on his desk.

'I know I'm not supposed to say this but you're a student – that's sort of what students do.'

'I don't like going out.'

'Why?'

'I don't know. I don't like it.'

'Do you have many friends?'

'Um, no.'

He swivelled his chair round to face me. I felt that familiar dizziness again. My mind began to drift out of my body and the painted sailing boat on the wall seemed to rock back and forth.

'Have you ever been diagnosed with depression or anxiety?'

'I saw a psychologist when I was a teenager but that was because I used to self-harm.'

'And now?'

'Not really.'

'Not really?'

'I don't self-harm as much.'

He gave me a stack of leaflets, some URLs that were

7

scribbled on Post-its and told me to have a read and get back to him. On my walk home I toyed with this new idea. Maybe I didn't have a terminal illness; maybe whatever I had was ... mental?

Whilst I had seen a psychologist as a teenager, those sessions were back in the Netherlands where I'm from. The term 'anxiety' had never been mentioned even though I do remember discussing the feeling. The word in its English form seemed floaty. I kind of knew what it was but not really. What actually *is* anxiety? What does it look like? How can you stop something you don't understand?

For me, anxiety is like having a crystal ball, but the ball is distorted and cloudy and everything in there is the most messed up version of events. For example, 'I can see that my future holds a work presentation and I bet I'll shit my pants and vomit on my boss and I'll never work in media ever again!'

The following week my doctor gave me the official diagnosis of 'generalised anxiety disorder'. Whilst coming to terms with anxiety as something I was dealing with, I realised how cruel a condition it is. Yes it's in your mind, but it feels extremely physical. My symptoms include sweating, trembling, heart palpitations and nausea. The nausea has always been my least favourite of the bunch; it's that horrible dragging feeling in the pit of my stomach that will stay long after the stressful event is over. It makes me feel like I'm constantly on the verge of puking but nothing will ever come out of my throat. At university the nausea developed into emetophobia (a fear of vomiting) and prevented me from showing up to classes, going to pubs and even just leaving the house. I was in permanent fear that I'd puke wherever I went. Sometimes I'd get on the bus only to have to get off again after one stop and walk home. I couldn't handle the rest of the twenty-minute journey.

I've also fainted and almost fainted a dozen times because of anxiety. I end up sending myself into such a whirlpool of worry and panic that my breathing spirals out of control, I feel dizzy, I start hyperventilating and BOOM I'm on the floor. Whilst I was never in any actual immediate danger (apart from the time I fainted at the hairdresser and she almost stabbed me in the head with her scissors), I genuinely believe that in that moment I am going to die. It's the thing people really underestimate about panic attacks. It's not a matter of 'just calm down'. You can't, because it feels like you're trapped inside your own body and the only escape is the relief you'll feel when the light finally goes out. You <u>will</u> die. There's no other option. It's terrifying.

9

But then when you do come out the other side you live in constant fear that it's going to HAPPEN AGAIN. Any hint of nausea, mild dizziness or a shaky hand and it's all systems go in my head. I imagine a bunch of army men running around preparing for battle: 'She's about to blow fellas! All hands on deck!' There's also that lingering feeling of shame after I survive an attack. When you were so certain you were about to die and yet you're still very much alive it can feel like a slight anti-climax. Not that I wanted to die but I'm embarrassed I genuinely thought I would and yet here I am. Blood pumping, heart racing.

I've had anxiety in places that were so mundane and boring I'd never expected my body to unleash such an extreme reaction. In an Asda in Bristol during the height of my anxiety I attempted a do a food shop with my boyfriend P. It was one of those enormous Asdas where it seems like there's an endless stream of garish lights dotting aisle after aisle after aisle. There's always a fear for me that in large supermarkets or shopping malls I'll get swallowed up: I'll be stuck in an aisle and never get out. Supermarkets feel like a mangled maze and there's no place to stop for a rest. You have to keep going, right to the till where, if you're not fast enough, you'll hold up all the people behind you.

P. walked ahead of me, ticking off the list of groceries I had meticulously made. Thanks to my fear of puking everywhere I didn't really socialise at uni so I had a lot of time to do things like make a joint food plan to last us a week. I'd organise the list in food groups making it easier to find items in the supermarket. I'd then calculate exactly how much everything would cost and split it down the middle so we'd each pay half. P. didn't really mind my food shopping dictatorship. It meant he saved money and didn't have to worry about what he was eating for dinner.

So we were in Asda and had only just made it to the fresh food section when I felt the panic set in. I stopped in my tracks. The bright supermarket lights seemed to merge together to form a wild tidal wave about to crash on top of me. I passed the shopping list to P. like we were soldiers in an epic war movie and I was handing over a picture of my wife and kids to my comrade before taking my last breath: 'Go forth, be brave and please tell my wife I love her.'

To the outside world I probably looked relatively normal. As P. went off into battle I decided to find an aisle that was less busy. I found the entertainment section and picked up one of Britney Spears's unofficial biographies whilst my vision blurred and turned to blue. I slumped to the ground but managed to hoist myself into a sitting position. I felt like everyone was staring at me so I grabbed the book and pretended to read. I sat there until P. collected me and we walked home. I felt defeated and silly and stupid and refused to talk about what had happened. I spent the rest of the evening in bed.

I've had other panic attacks in situations that were more unfortunate than Asda. My personal favourite being the one I had a year and a half after Asda-gate. P. and I had broken up. We'd been dating for eight years, and had grown up together and barely left each other's sides. I was alone now and I had no idea how all this worked, this dating stuff. How would I meet someone new?

I had the very unglamorous job of being an usher in a theatre in the West End. The Casanova of my colleagues, a guy I'll call R. – dark hair, suave – began to flirt with me. I could just about manage the flirting and reciprocated whenever I felt brave enough. When he eventually asked after a night in the pub if I wanted to go back to his I thought I'd received the golden ticket. This is what single life is like I cheered. Handsome guys ask you to go back to their house and you do that because you can – this is great!

Well, not really. Nerves cluttered my brain and I started to do that annoying thing I often do in the presence of men I want to impress where I hide away my personality and become a cardboard version of myself, hoping that I project whatever it is they want from me. 'Please like me please like me please like me,' pleaded my brain as we took the Tube back to his. A fight broke out in our carriage between a toothless man and a businessman in a grey suit. Allegedly, Toothless Man had had an accident and may or may not have shat himself. Businessman was screaming in his face telling him he was disgusting and should get off the train and go shower.

I really should have taken this as an omen for the night to come (don't worry, I didn't quite shit myself).

R. and I got into his flat and watched some *Alan Partridge*, which guys often like doing when they find out I'm foreign (it's that followed by *The Office* followed by *Fawlty Towers* followed by *Blackadder*). After this we retreated to his bedroom, where I focused on being a totally cool, sexy girl and not at all awkward or weird. This was my first time sleeping with someone new after eight years of being with the same person. What if my body was ugly? What if my vagina was weird? What if I smelt bad?

We got to it, which I know is a very unsexy way of describing sex, but I genuinely can't remember if it was any good because I was so goddamn stressed. When it was over he muttered something about not normally sleeping with people he's not properly dating and I said, 'Oh yeah, same,' even though what I meant to say was: 'Wait, what? What is happening? Is this a one-night thing? Do I go home? What do I do?' He shut his eyes and seemed to fall asleep immediately so I shut my eyes too. I somehow managed to sleep even though my body was so tense I was lying there like a corpse in a freezer.

I woke up in the middle of the night needing to pee. At the time he shared a flat with his sister and her now husband, which probably added to my nerves. The thought of bumping into them filled me with dread. Would I introduce myself? Would they think I was some floozy? Would they think I was an intruder? 'Just get the peeing over with and run back to the room,' I told myself. Seemed like a pretty simple plan until I'd made myself so tense and stressed out I couldn't pee. Nothing was happening, despite the fact that my bladder was achingly full. Horror struck. 'Fuck,' I thought, 'my bladder isn't working any more.'

I tried to think about running water, I turned the tap on and quietly started humming TLC's 'Waterfalls' but no luck. Here I was, butt naked on the loo apart from an old wrestling T-shirt R. had lent me, freaking out that my body was going to fill up with urine and eventually explode.

I decided to give up on the whole urinating thing. I felt dizzy and panicky and I needed to go back to the bed and lie down. I flushed anyway so no one would get suspicious and left the bathroom. Somewhere halfway down this tiny corridor the bones in my legs turned to mulch. Despite the darkness my vision became all dotted and turquoise. I just wanted to make it to the bedroom but my body wasn't working with me. Before I knew it I was on the floor and on my way down I'd managed to bash my cheek on his sister's bike. The poor guy ran out of his room and saw me sprawled across the carpet, at which point I raised a very meek don't-worry-it's-all-OK thumbs up.

He then sort of semi-dragged me back to his bedroom and put me to bed whilst I kept trying to tell him how sorry I was. With a throbbing cheek and a bladder full of pee I tried to force sleep on myself. I couldn't. Luckily it was 4am. I just needed to wait two more hours when it would be acceptable to leave. On leaving his house I gave him a high five and walked my way to Southfields train station. I got off halfway back to my house before finding a Starbucks to finally pee in. When I did it felt like I was peeing fire but it still felt good. The tension in my body eased a little.

To my great surprise R. and I ended up seeing each other again. After this escapade we even dated for a year and a bit. I learnt that things I consider to be END OF THE WORLD dramatic affairs really aren't so dramatic for other people. Fainting in someone's corridor isn't really that much of a big deal and in hindsight it's pretty funny.

Asda and post-sex panic attacks are two pretty extreme reactions I've had thanks to anxiety caused by generally not feeling comfortable in certain situations. On a day-to-day basis, anxiety can shapeshift and manifest itself in lots of different ways. It's a constant presence; a cloud that won't leave you alone, or a whisper in your ear that won't go away.

Here's what a bad anxiety day looks like:

- Waking up in the middle of the night to remember that thing I said five years ago that probably came across as a bit rude. Time to linger on that memory until sunrise!
- Waking up to mentally list all the people I'm pretty sure hate me and why they hate me and what would happen if I bumped into them in the street
- Leaving the house only to go back in again because it feels like a ton of bricks is falling down on my head
- Bopping my knee up and down so fast people walk by my desk to ask if I'm OK
- Having a bath to try to relax but then remembering the bath is basically an open coffin filled with my own liquid filth
- Hearing that voice in my head that follows me round and tells me what a pile of trash I am
- Laughing at something a co-worker says only to

then stop laughing because I sound like a goat
and people must hate the sound of me

- Having a nice time with someone whilst also being
convinced they secretly hate me
- Having to consult six friends about whether
that one text I sent one of our other friends
was perhaps a bit inappropriate and are we
absolutely 100 per cent positive they don't think
I'm a freak?
- When it's a bit humid outside and it feels like
oxygen is slowly being sucked out of the world
and there isn't enough and dear god why is
everyone else breathing freely like this?
- Having a knot of fear erupt at the base of
my spine, then shooting up my body until I'm
covered in a film of sweat and I have no idea why
my body is reacting like this because I was literally
just sitting here reading an email
- Seeing a pile of clothes in the dark and thinking it
looks like a massive panther, then thinking, 'Holy
shit, what if it *is* a panther?' followed by, 'Holy
shit, the fact that you think it's a panther means
you're probably losing your mind'
- Mentally saying goodbye to that guy you're
really enjoying spending time with because you'll
probably fuck it up anyway
- Receiving a very small amount of criticism at

work and, instead of dealing with it by doing better at the next task, spending the whole day Googling new jobs because this is it THEY WILL FIRE YOU

This is what a good anxiety day looks like:

- Getting up well rested because I was actually able to sleep
- Getting up and reading a book before I have to start the day because I've given myself enough time to slowly get out of bed and not bolt out the door
- Sitting in a meeting and not worrying about projectile vomiting on anyone
- Going for a swim not because I think my butt is too fat but because genuinely fancy moving my body
- Losing track of time on the Tube because I'm listening to a true crime podcast and I'm completely absorbed and not imagining death by stampede in the carriage
- Having lunch in the office canteen and being able to enjoy my cheese sandwich

because I don't feel like my head's about to disconnect from my body

- Tweeting something and not deleting it because I'm worried it's too lame/weird/annoying
- Going home and not drinking a bottle of wine by myself but instead making a meal that has actual vegetables in it
- Going home and not regretting 1,500 alleged mistakes I made that day
- Making a list of things I want to achieve over the rest of the year because I'm genuinely excited about the future
- Acknowledging that my body is not my enemy, it just overreacts to things sometimes and that's actually OK
- Texting a friend to make a plan without the fear that they'll inevitably cancel because who would want to hang out with me anyway?
- Tidying up my room because I want to live in a calm space, not on top of a mountain of clothes and dishes

I sort of have a handle on my day-to-day anxiety but I am yet to go back to Glastonbury. I have made progress though – after years of avoiding concerts, cinemas and plays I can get through a festival pretty much OK now. A lot of preparation has to take place and it's important

I'm around people I feel like I can trust and be honest with. If things get wobbly I have to be able to leave without feeling like I'm letting anyone down. I have to have plenty of water on me and ideally I prefer not to stand bang in the middle of a crowd.

Here are some other ways I've learnt how to survive a gig:

- I always find the more you know the band the better. When they're playing songs I know the words to I focus on the lyrics, sing at the top of my lungs and dance until my back is covered in sweat. It's when I'm not so familiar with the music that my mind wanders and starts thinking about fire or stampedes or gas explosions. Before any gig I check the set list they last played to be ahead of the game

- Have plenty of water on you. If they don't let you bring water into the venue head to the bar before you do anything else and get a decent supply. Stay hydrated!

- Bring gum. Super minty gum gives me something to focus on. It also grounds me and snaps me back to reality when dizziness starts to kick in

- Try not to fight the panic. Be kind to your body – it's not trying to ruin this experience for you. Tell yourself you're going to be OK

- Put your hands up – you can pretend it's because you're dancing but secretly you're giving your body a massive stretch, which will help relax your muscles
- Make sure you're not doing lots of little short breaths. Inhale for three counts, hold for three counts, then exhale for six. You could do this to the beat of the music if it lends itself to it. Disclaimer: I tried this at Blink-182 and it did not work
- If you're sweating and you have any of that water left, pour some on your head. You'll look really hardcore, trust me
- Lastly, don't feel like you have to be in the thick of the crowd. Let your gig buddies know you like to stand near the exit. Do your own thing. Make sure you're comfortable

OH WAIT, IT'S NOT JUST ANXIETY . . .

University signalled the time I learnt about anxiety and its effects on my life but there was more. A few weeks after the GP told me he suspected I had an anxiety disorder I went back for a check-up and he added one more part to it: 'We think you are depressed too.'

I've always found depression incredibly hard to describe because it's such a mystery. It exists on its own terms and there's nothing quite like it. What I *do* know is that it made me feel trapped; the same way anxiety makes me feel trapped but heavier, stickier and more impenetrable. Everything is shrouded in the negative view that I have about myself, my friends, my work, everything. Any moments of joy are short-lived and are quickly spoiled by a bitter fluid. Whilst I feel like there's an external pressure, hot and heavy, pressing down on my skull, inside I feel empty and hollow. The only sound I can hear is my own heart beating, taunting me for still being alive.

My depression coexists with anxiety and sometimes the scales tip. When depression takes over the lights go out. This isn't to say that anxiety is easier to live with, but I have been able to at least attempt productive coping mechanisms when it comes to anxiety. Depression makes that harder. 'What's the point in coping mechanisms?' I whisper to myself in a dark room. 'I shouldn't really be here anyway.'

In my third year of uni I became obsessed with the idea of disappearing. I wanted to stop living but I didn't have the energy to do anything about it. Instead, I'd lie in bed staring at the ceiling and imagine walking for days until atom by atom my body started to vanish. The more I'd walk, the more I'd disappear. I longed to be transparent. No blood or gore. No corpse of myself lying around for someone else to clear up. No one would be too traumatised. I could text everyone saying I'm absolutely fine, I just decided to exit stage left and never come back again. No biggie.

When anxiety and depression decide to merge and come at me in unison it's like my body is being moved in two different directions. Anxiety wants me to freak out, panic, run around to get help and call everyone I know, whilst depression locks my bones in place and tells me to stay put. On the one hand my body is heavy and sluggish; on the other it's whizzing around and unravelling because of the pressure I've put on myself to get it together, be normal and just get on with things.

Anxiety and depression held hands the day I decided to walk to the top of Bristol's Park Street and across to Brandon Hill and sit on the bench made famous by the TV series *Skins*. It was 5pm, no one was there. I imagined most people were in pubs, chatting about their days and weekend plans. I hated myself for being so completely alone in a city with tons of students and a boyfriend who I was living with. Why was I *this* lonely? Why did I not make an effort with anyone? Why was I such a loser? I became a detective putting myself under a harsh light trying to get to the bottom of why I was so impossibly alone.

Instead of approaching my predicament with a bit of self-sympathy I felt angry and ashamed of being me. My anxiety had convinced me that everyone on my course hated me because I was weird and stupid, whilst my depression told me that they didn't hate me at all. I hated them. I was a judgemental asshole that hated anyone having a good time. I deserved to feel this isolated. I was a bitch.

I looked down at the view below my bench and imaged flinging myself down it. Anyone who knows Bristol knows it's impossible to kill yourself on Brandon Hill – it's not a cliff. Worst case you'd end up doing a body roll to one of the paths where the road evens out where you'd come to a halt and someone would give you a strange look. It just seemed enticing. To let my body go. To flop it over the hill and roll until I'd stop rolling and maybe after my brain had rattled around my skull it would snap out of its turmoil.

I tried to summon some extra energy from a pocket of my brain. Something that would get me off this bench, stop fantasising about tumbling down the hill like a human sausage roll and just go home. Go write something. Go shower. Go talk to someone. Go do something productive. Anxiety whizzed around my head telling me to get off my ass whilst depression sat on top of my skull like a helmet that's too tight.

I saw a toddler run down the hill into the arms of her dad. She had on a red bomber jacket and an orange woolly hat and was running down with carefree abandon. She shrieked. Joy made her skin glow. I got up and wiped the frustrated tears that had fallen out of my eye balls. I steadied my feet, took a deep breath and exhaled a high-pitched scream whilst I tried to run without restraint. I ran all the way down. Trying not to worry about tripping. 'Just run. Just keep running,' I told myself. Then I got to the bottom. I looked behind me. Cabot Tower was staring down at me. The toddler was gaping at me. The dad ushered her away. I left the park and burst out laughing to myself.

This running down the hill incident wasn't some big turning point; I didn't run my way into the sweet arms of recovery. I think what it illustrated was a tiny little turning point, a tiny little injection of life, of weirdness, of wanting to live unashamedly. I've been lucky enough to have a few of these moments. There have been so many times in my life where I'm sitting on a bench or standing on the edge of a platform or lying in a bath clutching a razor blade thinking about how great it would be to extinguish myself. To disappear. And then there's always something, a small feeling, a tiny spark of electricity, that says 'No.' It's what walks me to A&E; it's what takes me to my doctor's waiting room; and it's what encourages me to go to therapy and support meetings. That tiny spark makes sure I don't have sharp objects in my room or that I go home when things get too much. That spark keeps me going, and stops me from disappearing completely.

How to find that little spark in your own self when the lights go out:

- Write your thoughts down. It doesn't have to be in full diary form, it can be incoherent or just an angry scribble. This will help keep your mind from running around in circles in its own cage. Set the words free
- Make a playlist of songs that make you feel something within your whole body: it might be classical, it might be deep house, it might be jazz. I like Bikini Kill and Radiohead and old-school Mariah Carey. I like songs that absorb me, songs I can lose myself in, songs that take me away somewhere else – even if it's just for a moment
- Stretch your body out. When I stretch I feel good. It doesn't have to be a proper arch your back and lick your asshole type stretch they like to do in

yoga, just anything that moves your body in a different way. Feel your body, acknowledge that you have it and it's good to you

- Go outside. Even if you sit on a bench or on the grass or on a stoop. Go outside. Breathe fresh air
- Move your body. After you've stretched it put it into motion. Jump, skip, walk, jog – and ideally scream whilst you do it
- Lastly, remember that you're made up of 70,000,00 0,000,000,000,000,000,000,000 atoms. My depression makes me feel small, insignificant and hollow. I'm not hollow. Not really. I'm filled with organs and skin and mucus and blood that's full of life

REMEMBER THIS
WHEN YOU'RE SCARED OF
YOUR OWN BRAIN

I've often felt like I have no control over my mind. It goes down corridors I don't want it to go down. It punishes me, challenges me and, quite frankly, freaks me the fuck out. It's frustrating because my mind lives in my own head, so how can something inside me be working against me in that way?

As a child I often fantasised about drilling a hole in my scalp to let all the bad parts out. Being afraid of your own thoughts is entrapping. It's like walking around with explosives built into your brain but someone else is carrying the trigger. You don't know where they are or when they'll hit the button.

Learning about my brain and what is behind the things

that scare me helped me come to terms with my own head. Knowing about the cause and effect of certain symptoms grounds them in biology – they're still annoying and frustrating but I'm not as alarmed.

The first is dissociation. Dissociation is described by the American Psychiatric Association as 'a disruption in the usually integrated functions of consciousness, memory, identity, or perception of the environment'. It's often a reaction to overpowering stress. For me, it's like my mind folds in on itself. I'm there, but I'm not really there.

There are two strands to dissociation. One is depersonalisation, which is often described as a feeling of watching yourself from a distance. The very first therapist I saw as a teenager used to call this 'Helicopter Maggy': I'm in a helicopter looking down on whatever it is that I'm doing, often full of judgement and scorn. My school boyfriend used to play in a band and I'd go to every gig despite the fact that I never knew anyone and hated crowded bars. I'd often stand there and that helicopter would kick in: 'Look at that stupid girl, she has no friends, she's so dumb, she can't talk to anyone.' I'd then start to tear down everything about myself: my hair, the way I was standing, the way my arms hung loosely next to my body. It meant I could never relax or even enjoy the music. I was my own paparazzi, hovering over myself, putting that horrible self-critical voice on loudspeaker.

The other strand of dissociation is derealisation where you feel disconnected from reality. Often in a high school movie when the protagonist's love interest is seen kissing someone else time appears to stand still. Shocked, the protagonist watches the horrible events unfold in slow motion. For me, derealisation feels like that, only there's no sad indie music playing in the background. I feel spaced out and floaty. People's voices sound far away; mouths appear to move out of synch with sound.

There are lots of reasons why people experience dissociation, from trauma to an inability to process emotional information. Often it's your brain protecting your body from perceived threat. For me, the safest space has always been in my own head. That's where everything takes place. I've always been content sitting by myself playing out conversations and scenarios. Even now, if I need a break from something I'll lie down, shut my eyes and go somewhere peaceful to mull my ideas over.

Whilst it's natural for me when I feel unsafe to retreat to the place I know best, it's not a very comfortable experience, especially when I have no control over it. I've described it often as having my head trapped in a fishbowl. I can see things but it's all a bit misshapen and the sounds feel echoey. I want to smash the bowl so badly and be present but I can't. The more I think about it the thicker the glass of the bowl seems to become.

My dissociation has made it difficult for me to always

act in a way that I want to, especially in social situations. For example, in a pub meeting a boyfriend's friends for the first time, I want to be outgoing and fun. I want to sound interesting and interested in everything everyone else has to say, when all of a sudden it's impossible for me to string a sentence together. The words that come out of my mouth are all garbled and weird. Why can't I just function normally?

Parts of my self-destructive behaviours are to do with wanting to get out of that fishbowl. I often hope that by causing myself physical or emotional pain it'll act like someone's chucking a bucket of ice water on me to get me out of a nightmare. I try it with alcohol too. The soft rocking feeling I get after a few large glasses of white wine mimics the weird dreamy feeling of dissociation. They almost mirror each other. It's like I'm sinking into myself but pulling up a chair at the same time. I'm here to stay. It feels nice here.

As well as dissociation, intrusive thoughts that feel more like voices or urges often bombard my brain. Intrusive thoughts are so common that you'd be more of an anomaly if you *didn't* experience them. They're like a little fire you can't put out. They are incredibly persistent and can be quite scary. In the book *Abnormal Psychology: An Integrative Approach* some of the most common intrusive thoughts are broken down into causing harm to yourself (jumping out of a window) or to someone else (dropping your friend's baby), contamination (catching a disease from a dirty toilet seat), doing something inappropriate (randomly getting up in a meeting to swear at your boss) or safety (thinking you've left the oven on after you leave the house).

For some people, the occurrence and intensity of intrusive thoughts are so powerful they develop their own coping strategies simply to get through the day. The solution to distressing thoughts is never as simple as 'just don't think about it' – if only! To prove how impossible it is a social psychologist called Daniel Wegner conducted the following experiment. He asked participants to verbalise whatever it was they were thinking at that very moment for five minutes. The only rule: they had to try their very best not to think about a fluffy white bear. If the white bear did pop into their heads, they had to ring a bell. Despite explicit instructions to avoid thinking about the bear, participants obviously thought about it. In fact, more than once per minute (on average).

Similarly, I find the more I tell myself not to think about something the more I'm likely to think of that very thing. Suppressing my intrusive thoughts only seems to make them thrive. I might be sitting at the back of the bus trying to calm my anxiety down a bit because it's busy and fogged up inside from bad weather. I'm just about coping when a little light flickers in my brain that says: 'Wouldn't now be *such* a bad time to yell "I'VE GOT A BOMB!?" And there we have it. Not only am I nervous because the bus is filled to the brim with humans, I'm now convincing myself that I'm

teetering on the edge of madness, coaxing myself to be a pretend terrorist which will inevitably freak the hell out of these innocent people. I follow the thought all the way through to getting arrested, facing a hearing, losing my job, having my parents be disappointed and having my boyfriend explain to his friends that his girlfriend is in prison because she thought it would be hilarious to shout 'BOMB!' on a bus. I'd lose everything in an instant. I shouldn't do it. But maybe I should? No. Don't do it. But what *if*?

Feel exhausted yet?

So much of our day is spent being mentally active that we come to rely on our mind to work the way we want it to. However, sometimes our train of thought goes down an unwanted path conjuring up a reaction that's both unwelcome and perhaps even harmful.

When I'm depressed, every single thing around me becomes a tool to hurt myself with. An impulse tells me to stand closer to the platform, to smash my face into a mirror, to down a whole bottle of bleach or run in front of a car. It's exhausting and it colonises so much of the good in my life.

I've even had intrusive thoughts creep in right before or during sex. Right as I'm about to come my brain challenges me to think: 'What would be the most inappropriate image to conjure up right now?' Then images will flash, maybe a dead relative, – a maggot-infested carcass or suddenly I'll begin to recall some of the horrific images I've seen on the news. Then when I finally come I can convince myself I'm an absolute psychopathic nightmare. You come to an image of bloodshed and violence. YOU'RE A FREAK.

People with intrusive thoughts, especially people who have Obsessive Compulsive Disorder (OCD), often develop repetitive actions or compulsions to try and stop the intrusions from happening. Compulsions are things you do to try to make the obsessive irrational thoughts go away. Everyone's coping strategies are unique to them but often compulsions fall into these categories:

- Checking (repeatedly checking the appliances, blood pressure, locks)
- Repeating (rereading the same sentence, writing the same word, tapping)
- Counting (steps, bricks, numbers out loud)
- Washing (ritualised bathing, cleaning, brushing)

- Ordering (books, clothes, dishes)
- Physical (biting nails to all line up, blinking, shrugging)

Depending on where I was in my life I had different compulsions to manage intrusive thoughts. In uni I was living with my boyfriend P. who I'd come to fully depend on. When I felt him slipping away from me I became obsessed with the idea that he'd walk out of our flat and die, or even worse that I might accidentally kill him. The idea of losing him was so painful to me that I couldn't stop thinking about that very thing. I developed weird compulsions and rituals that I felt I had to carry out to make sure he'd be safe. One involved having to kiss him back three times if he ever kissed me on the lips. Some were more sexual and others had more to do with our flat: how the pillows were positioned and the arrangement of our books and DVDs.

My compulsions were starting to dictate my life and they were causing me to get sucked into a strange, very isolated state where I felt I couldn't live without P. It wasn't some form of romantic desperation, it was larger than me, than us: he was my life support. In my head I couldn't breathe without him. The pressure this put on P. was incredibly unfair. Every time he met up with someone else I took this as an extreme form of rejection, which made it worse. It also meant that I put no faith in myself. I didn't see myself as whole. I was only ever someone's girlfriend, and not a great one at that.

A lot of my intrusive thoughts are visual: they appear as single images that flash over and over again. Most often it'll have something to do with the body or something horrific I saw online. I am one of those people who will see a click-baity headline along the lines of 'ONLY WATCH THIS CYST VIDEO IF YOU'RE NOT SQUEAMISH' and, just to prove the headline wrong, I'll watch it, often with one eye closed. Some I can handle, especially when the headline oversells what's happening on screen. Others leave me feeling sick. When there are gross itty-bitty things coming out of people's skin I have to find that part on my own body and rub it at least nine times – making sure there are no itty-bitty things stuck in mine.

Sometimes my visual intrusions make me laugh. I want to shake my head and say: come on brain, not now OK! But there was a time when these images appeared so often and were so persistent I lived in fear that I was losing my mind. I had one counsellor, a very timid, kind-hearted Irish woman who worked at my university, who gave me a handy trick. It involves: *Club Penguin*.

In case you've never heard of it, *Club Penguin* was a multiplayer online game (it got the boot earlier this year). My younger brother was very into it growing up and I used to watch what he was up to over his shoulder. There's a bit where you dress up your penguin avatar, which for me was always the best part. You can dress them up in Converse, shades, concert T-shirts, dinosaur costumes, trucker caps, blonde wigs – the options are enjoyably endless.

When I was at uni I hadn't really thought about *Club Penguin* in years. At this time my anxiety was hellish and a medley of panic attacks and intrusive thoughts was becoming an almost hourly occurrence. I completely isolated myself to avoid having these episodes in public.

Freaky creepy crawlies under my skin hijacked most of my thoughts. I was obsessed. The fear wouldn't leave me alone. It popped up when I was in the shower, making food, reading a book or on the bus. I stopped being able to look at my own body. I just imagined creepy crawlies under there. I scratched my skin raw just to make sure there was nothing there but it didn't help. I'd tell myself to 'just not think about it', but that only made it come back ten fold.

I decided to quarantine myself out of the shame that my brain couldn't let go of this stupid irrational bug fear. I thought if it struck me when I was out or in a lecture or talking to someone in the corridor I'd probably show it on my face. Maybe I'd feel sick and vomit all over someone? I couldn't let that happen. I had to protect myself from the outside world and protect them from me. Only problem: I had a counselling appointment in a campus that was a ten-minute bus ride away. I knew I had to go. Something cracked a bit in my mind and I needed help. My self-induced quarantine was not a permanent solution.

I tackled that bus ride like I was heading into war. I armed myself with my tools: water, chewing gum, a book, a French language audio tape and some crackers. It was in the heat of the summer which didn't help but I managed to get a seat by an open window and the cool breeze felt like an escape route should I need one. I kept switching from book to audio tape to breathing deeply, all the while pushing the bug image down like I was trying to drown it in a puddle. It wouldn't die though. It was testing me.

Miraculously, I got to my appointment and sat down in a sticky fake-leather chair that was even more uncomfortable now that it was so warm. My counsellor asked: 'What's been happening to you this week?' I tried to swallow the big ball of shame that was rising up in my throat. I didn't want her to judge me or to think I was properly losing my shit but I knew I needed to tell someone about my thoughts. I really needed some help.

I told her about the bugs under the skin. We'd been talking about intrusive thoughts before so the foundation was there for us to be able to discuss it without me grappling for the right words. She asked me to properly describe everything about the image but as I did so I began to squirm in my chair. I started rubbing my arms and clenching my fists. She told me to stop and what seemed very out of the blue then said, 'Have you ever heard of *Club Penguin*?' I was zapped out of my discomfort. The randomness of the question threw me but also instantly reminded me of my brother who lived back home in the Netherlands and I missed him so much.

'Yes. I mean I never played it but my little brother loves that game. I've seen him on it a lot.'

'OK, good. Do you remember that bit where you can dress your penguin?'

I knew exactly what she was describing. The brilliant thing about *Club Penguin* is that its interface is so friendly and bright it easily sticks in your mind. I visualised that part of the game and the little wardrobe that pops up on the side.

My counsellor then told me to imagine myself in that image that I found so troubling – bugs crawling everywhere and my skin bursting open from all those critters squirming about. She told me to focus on my arm in particular but then imagine that arm in *Club Penguin* mode. Dress the arm up in a funny hat, she said. Put a moustache on it, or an armband, or a cap, or a wedding dress. Part of me was thinking, 'What the fuck is this?' and another part obeyed her. My arm detached itself from me, mentally, and fully immersed itself into the game. It wasn't something that was scaring me anymore, it was funny, kinda cute and totally harmless. I pictured all the little bugs and gave them hats too. I felt less threatened and grossed out.

I wouldn't say this technique is a magical cure – I can't dress up all my anxieties in a pink cowboy hat and suddenly feel great about my life – but particularly for intrusive visual images it helps me put my own spin on them, make them less scary. I spend a lot of time on the internet, on forums and threads. Almost every day I'll see something that makes me go, 'OH NOOO!' Sometimes it won't affect me and sometimes it'll stick with me for the whole day but at least I know it won't ruin my life.

One of my favourite times using the *Club Penguin* technique was when I was harbouring a lot of paranoia about a manager at work who had it in for me. Big chunks of my paranoia were justified: she used to schedule meetings deliberately when I couldn't make them, avoid eye contact with me in group discussions or say hi to everyone on our bank of desks but me. My anxiety about her trying to fire me escalated into random flashes of her trying to club me to death at work with a hammer (yep, thanks brain for making a shitty situation even shittier). I got up once to make a coffee and I could feel her walking behind me.

My brain quickly conjured up an image of her walking close to me, hammer in hand, about to strike and it made my heart rate go up. I distanced myself from the image, tried to look at it from above and turned her body into a massive white marshmallow. Instead of her charging towards me she was bouncing around the office like a big Jigglypuff. It made me chuckle and I was able to make my coffee in peace (and even manage a courteous 'hello' when our paths crossed).

The difficulty with intrusive thoughts is that the more I try to block them the louder they become. It feels like yelling at an incoming freight train and every time you yell 'STOP' it's only coming in closer. Instead of shouting 'Stop!' or 'Go away!' I've learnt to try to say other things. If, like me, you've been a bit of a sucker for self-help books you might have come across the saying 'This Too Shall Pass'. It's a little bit of a cliché, but when you strip all that away the core of the saying can feel incredibly true in a moment you need it the most. Whatever turmoil you're going through it's going to be over at some point – nothing is permanent (apart from maybe the blue butterfly tattoo on my forearm). Whilst there might be more turmoil awaiting you round the corner, you'll deal with that when you get there and once you do, it'll be over too. When I'm struck by an avalanche of negative thinking

I tell myself that it will pass, that it will wash over me, that this state I'm in isn't forever.

Even stars that seem to live in the sky forever flare up and eventually exhaust their fuel and collapse back into darkness. This probably sounds melancholic, but it reminds me that permanence really is an illusion. My panic attacks make me feel like I'm being burnt up. Heat flashes across my body. I get rashy and dizzy but, despite the fact that every time I've had an attack I've assumed this would be it for me and I'll be trapped in this hell forever, the burning subsides. My eyesight goes back to normal. The heat dies down and I can breathe again. It's so important to hang onto the fact that it's not forever. It will pass and I will make it out to the other side each time.

Another nifty trick I've adopted to combat panic and intrusive thoughts is to talk back to them – not just yell 'Stop!' but to actually have a bit of a conversation. The voice doing the talking isn't a voice that belongs to me, it's the voice of someone I love, respect, admire and makes me feel eternally calm. That voice is Oprah.

Oprah is a legend and an icon. She is arguably the most influential and powerful woman in the world and what makes her so enticing as a 'voice of reason' in my head is that she oozes empathy. In fact, it's part of her show, her persona and how she's always interacted with guests and audience members. She always felt to me like a badass nurturing grandmother, dishing up chicken soup and life-changing advice at the same time. The version of her that has developed in my head thrives because it listens. Even if my mind is going a hundred miles an hour, the 'Oprah' voice will slow it down and unpick it.

It helps even more if I imagine myself as a guest on her show. When I'm on the London underground, which is hellishly busy at the best of times, and I can feel that sense of panic starting to rise, I pretend we're talking about what I'm going through. It helps if I speak as someone who has been through it and survived, so instead of going, 'OPRAH, OMG THIS TUBE IS SO BUSY HELP!', I'm saying to her, 'Yes, I used to really struggle with panic attacks on the Tube but now I'm OK, I can manage.' Being on my own imagined version of her show allows me to visualise myself on the other side. I've been through the panic and I'm out of there now.

If I feel like I want to prevent what I can imagine might be a panic-triggering situation I'll go on her show and talk about something more general. Maybe about how stupid some of my ex-boyfriends are or how well my movie is doing (it's important to note that fictional me has not only survived panic attacks she's also got at least five Oscars). Having Oprah weigh in on my life, even if it's a slightly fictionalised version, is soothing and distracts me from the hoards of tourists flooding the platform at Oxford Circus.

Oprah or *Club Penguin*, they're both part of my

intrusive thought fight plan. I call on them like Zordon from *Power Rangers* when he gets all their watches beeping and they need to report for duty. Sometimes, though, the intrusive fight plan isn't enough and I need a real outside voice that's not just in my own head. Whilst I've always felt proud of being self-sufficient and able to get on with things alone, when I'm stuck in a feedback loop of hell I need someone outside of my body to snip the loop. Sometimes it's with their own opinion whilst other times their opinion spawns a different viewpoint in my own head and I'm able to climb out of the quicksand.

This outside voice is often my therapist or a good friend. It's important to me that it's someone I trust. The nature of my intrusive thoughts is that they're on repeat. So having someone say, 'Don't worry, there are no bugs crawling around your skin' isn't really enough to make them stop. Three minutes later I'm going to have to ask them again and this might repeat throughout the day. It's key I don't feel ashamed or judged or that my friend is running out of patience.

The whole nature of my mental feedback loop is that it's tricky to unshackle yourself in one swift swoop. It takes time and it's always going to want to drag you back in. I might have approached a friend with a problem. Even something practical and simple like: I don't know what to do about the fact that my rent is increasing next month. They might help me reach a logical conclusion that I agree with but one moment later I can feel myself sinking into that same problem, with all the different options, scenarios and potential outcomes swarming around my head like bees. I can see how it might be frustrating for that other person when I'm back to where I was at the beginning of our conversation, but repetition is key. I need to hear their advice more than once. It's like they're tossing me a lifebelt when I'm drowning at sea but it might take a few tries before I'm able to cling on.

A lot of my techniques fall under an idea called 'mindfulness'. Mindfulness belongs to a school of Buddhist meditation. Professor Jon Kabat-Zinn who founded the MBSR (mindfulness-based stress reduction) programme defines it as a non-judgemental awareness of the present moment, through focusing attention intentionally on the moment-by-moment experience. For me, this translates to viewing my intrusive thoughts and acknowledging that they're there without getting annoyed, scared or angry at myself for the fact that they're there. Imagine you're lying in a field looking up at the sky and you're watching the clouds go by without passing any judgement. The clouds aren't bad or good, they're just clouds. You're seeing them detached from any emotional reaction you might have. You're giving your mind space to view something just as it is without making up your mind immediately.

I once had a big batch of intrusive thoughts break out

whilst I was in the middle of a company-wide meeting. The meeting involved a fancy presentation that thankfully I didn't have to take any part in. The three company bosses were giving a big speech about how much the new sales team had brought in. I was annoyed at myself because there had been free pizza in the middle of the room and I had conveniently sat myself next to it. When people started pouring into the room they all went for the pizza and huddled in the same position. Soon enough I felt like I was in the middle of an onion and the rings around me were all the other people. I was about to get up to move but the bosses came in and the talk started. I told myself to stay put so I wouldn't cause a big scene.

As the talk went on I got more and more panicky. I thought, what if I really need to pee, what if I need to vomit, what if I need to shit? How will I get up? How will I survive this? The more I thought about how I couldn't escape the room unnoticed the more I really wanted to. My thoughts were getting stronger and stronger and nothing seemed to quieten them down. Even Oprah was nowhere to be seen. Instead of suppressing them I took a deep breath and tried to hear what they were saying.

To be honest they sounded like a gaggle of irrational children in a supermarket trolley: 'MUM GIVE ME THAT ICE CREAM NOW!' I listened though and didn't think about how they were making me feel emotionally. Instead I paid attention to what was happening to me physically. I focused on my stomach where I felt queasy from anxiety but nothing indicated that I was going to eject stomach bile everywhere as my thoughts were suggesting. I inhaled and filled my body with air. I exhaled and the nausea subsided a little. I was onto something. I was calmly breathing through the stress. I was noticing what was happening and listening to my thoughts like a helpful bystander or perhaps a scientist observing a simple experiment in the microscope beneath his eye.

When our CEO stopped talking I realised I'd made it to the end of the presentation. People started filing out of the room. It was 5pm on a Friday, which is akin to it being the last day of school before the summer. Everyone dashed around me and grabbed a free beer from the fridge. I felt I was somewhere else, somewhere better. I was secretly incredibly proud of myself. For sitting through the presentation, for sitting with my thoughts. Yes, it was awful and I did think I was going to hurl for a bit there, but I was able to calm myself down. I felt like I'd just jumped out of a plane and landed safely on the ground: I did it. I was chuffed. I even remember giving myself a little squeeze.

In these situations you need to give yourself a little mental boost but it's hard to say, 'You go girl!' to yourself when you don't really believe it. If you're anything like me you're probably quite allergic to clichés, especially in the style of anything you might see plastered on someone's Instagram with a soft pink background and Moonflower font. However, sometimes I need a helping hand and sometimes that helping hand comes in the form of a mantra. So here are some not-so-cringeworthy (I hope!) mantras that help me when my brain needs to chill the fuck out:

- The battle cry: All right anxiety, we got this, GIVE ME YOUR WORST
- The good advice: Remember you went through this before and you can go through this again
- The distraction: 'Look at this stuff ... Isn't it neat ... ?' Or sub this for whatever Disney song you know totally off by heart. If you find yourself somewhere you can belt it out loud even better!
- The reward: When this is over we're getting pizza
- The Hogwarts' chant: Those patient Hufflepuffs are true and unafraid of toil (or whatever your House description is!)
- The football coach speech: Don't try and get over it, walk through it
- Or even better: 'Clear eyes, full hearts, can't lose' – from *Friday Night Lights* (if you haven't watched this show

49

definitely do – you'll get a wealth of brand new motivation!)

- The song from the musical *Avenue Q*: 'Everything in life is only for now'
- The mindfulness quote: You can't stop the waves, but you can learn to surf (even though I probably can't because I have no balance, so maybe I'll learn how to bodyboard)
- The badass cheer: Feel the fear and do it anyway. I stole this from Dr Susan Jeffer's book, which is all about being more assertive
- The happy memory: Remember that time you were eight and you entered a school talent show on your own and you were so scared you almost peed your pants but you got through it and fucking won!
- The power ballad: 'At first I was afraid, I was petrified' and then I fast forward straight to 'I will surviiiive'
- This piece of advice from *Gone with the Wind*: 'After all, tomorrow is another day'
- And lastly this less profound piece of advice aimed at my anxiety, not myself: 'Shut your fucking face, uncle fucka.' Thank you *South Park*!

HOW TO FIND OUT WHAT TRIGGERS YOU

I'm hypersensitive to just about anything. I always imagine my brain to be naked, completely vulnerable to every single stimulus around it. I genuinely don't think it's all bad. I have A LOT of feelings; some not very useful, but some are fun. Movies become visceral experiences where I'm rooting for the character so much I can completely lose myself. It's also made me a good listener. When someone's telling me a story I always feel like I'm totally there with them, clinging onto their every word. I also feel like I'm quite perceptive. I've often been the first to uncover office gossip just by noticing people's little mannerisms: the slightly tense way they walk out of meeting rooms (yep, they're going to quit) or the two co-workers who always gently nudge each other's shoulders when they walk past each other's desk (definitely banging).

On the negative side, being hypersensitive means a lot of things have the potential to send me into a bad spell: a particular song, a word, a shrug, an item of food. A little blip can make me redefine my great day to, 'WHY THE FUCK DID I BOTHER TO GET UP?' When I think about triggers it feels like there are too many to name. I've thought about encasing myself in a bubble, like Bubble Boy, but instead of protecting myself against germs I'm protecting myself against triggers.

Someone once told me a story about a camel in London Zoo (hang in there, this is relevant). Every day this camel goes for a guided walk around the zoo so guests can enjoy seeing it up close. Before the camel goes for a walk one of the other zookeepers goes ahead and makes sure that the route is as close to what the route looked like the day before as possible. If there's an overflowing bin, it'll be removed. If there's an umbrella bopping around that's too bright the owner will be asked to put it down. Basically, if the camel sees anything that's too out of the ordinary it'll freak out. Everything needs to be the same.

I can relate to this camel. Whilst it would be super boring, life as a simple and safe routine that I could repeat over and over would mean I'd be free from triggers. I wouldn't self-harm or experience bouts of rage or misery. Thing is, life really isn't like this, and for good reason. Your experiences are often muddy and complicated and subject to random changes and challenges. The best way to avoid triggers is to figure out what they actually are. What makes me feel uncomfortable and what drives me to the edge?

I need to see things laid out in front of me to be able to have them sink into my brain. I was a visual learner in school. I had to plaster maths equations and history facts on my walls to be able to memorise them. If this strikes a chord with you, you might find having some sort of visual account of your moods very helpful. Long live the journal!

'Journaling' is a bit of a trendy buzzword, but the act of keeping a diary dates back to the second century AD. Type 'bullet journal' into a search engine and you'll see how many people are reaping its benefits. In simple terms, this is a handy organisation system with a set of signs and signals that you can decide on and use how you want. It's a mix between a to-do list, notebook and diary and essentially helps you to manage your time. On top of this you can use it to track your thoughts, mood, activities, big events, small events, tasks and deadlines, and how these might all feed into your mental and physical health.

I struggled a bit with returning to diary writing because it reminded me so much of being an angsty teen, scribbling down overly emotional poetry, declaring my love for some guy who sat behind me in class. However, I've come to see journaling as something that's very grown-up, sensible and ultimately very useful.

The thing I've enjoyed the most about journaling is that it's like a social media platform but for myself (so an anti-social platform). I use it to both look forward and to look back. I'll make my weekly plan but I'll also stick in theatre tickets or quotes or lyrics from songs I've been enjoying. My journal is a scrapbook of all the things that have made me feel good and a planner for all the things I'll do to carry on that feeling.

There are lots of different methods for tackling the organisational part of bullet journaling. Don't fall into the trap of having to make it look 'pretty'. There are loads of Instagram accounts dedicated to all the intricate doodles people do in their journals: little symmetrical check boxes and stunningly drawn banners. Thing is, no one is going to see your journal (unless you want them to) so who cares what it looks like? It just has to make sense to you, that's all.

Journaling has helped me to slow my life down a level. When I feel like I'm in the centre of a whirlpool and life is the water thrashing round and round, stepping back makes it calm down for a bit. Jotting down my problems, what I need to tackle and what needs my immediate attention makes everything more manageable.

I also found a lot of value in tracking moods so I can start to think about what might be causing some of them. I give my day a number out of ten for 'tiredness', 'sadness', 'anger', etc. To no one's surprise, PMS causes a lot of those numbers to go up but apart from that I found that whilst I *had* cut down drinking I hadn't really cut down enough. I was still drinking more than a bottle of wine three times a week which was making me wake up miserable. I wasn't sleeping enough and every time I met up with my boyfriend at the time I'd end up stressed out and frustrated. I needed to make some big life adjustments but I was too stuck in the middle to see exactly what needed to change.

If you feel tracking, scrapbooking and journaling is something you might like to try, you should splash out on a bitchin' diary. If it's not colourful or 'you' enough customise it with wrapping paper or magazine clippings. Make this space totally yours. Mine is as garish and weird-looking as my MySpace page in 2005 and that's exactly how I like it.

KEEP TRACK OF WHAT MAKES YOU FEEL GOOD

Instead of just thinking about what makes me miserable, I started tracking the little everyday things that boost my mood. If I'm at work, which, let's face it, we all are most of the time, and I can feel the pull of self-doubt, I make sure I leave my desk to go out for lunch. Perhaps I'll read my book under a tree or go for a little walk. If I have enough time I'll make myself a quick playlist of angsty folk songs.

To help you discover what your little pick-me-ups might be, try to keep a note of them. Think of it like you're assembling a toolkit; once you've experienced something that acted as a little mood booster add it to the kit. You can turn to it when things take a bad turn.

Sometimes your toolkit is going to work wonders, other times it might not. Unfortunately, when I'm in a bad mood because I've had to pay a shitty tax bill I'm not necessarily going to feel better because I read my book for a bit. Some things are just universal mood killers. Despite that, having a collection of options to turn to when I'm lost or adrift is comforting. I've made a list of some of these things below hopefully they might inspire you to list some of your own:

● Finding a band I'd never heard of before on Spotify and being blown away

- Bonus points if they happen to be playing in town soon
- Showing a friend a great pic I took of them and for a second they actually see themselves as the wonderful ray of sunshine and beauty that I see them as
- Even better when they make that photo their new profile pic
- Waking up early at the weekend just to lie in bed and enjoy all the time I still have left to sleep
- Giving a lot of unworn clothes to the charity shop and feeling like I've shed a lot of excess skin
- Rescuing a seemingly dead plant in my bedroom and giving it a new lease of life
- Reading a really dense and wordy article in a scientific journal but actually sort of getting it
- Running for the bus, making it and not feeling like death on a stick because I haven't been smoking as much that week
- Bonus when the bus driver smiles in a way that says 'congrats' but also 'don't worry, would've waited for you anyway'
- Going for a brisk walk in the winter and feeling the cold hair rush in and out of me like it's purifying my lungs
- Walking home after a yoga class when my shoulder stand was maybe three per cent better than it was last time

- Catching someone's eye when it's weird chanty time in that yoga class and you both laugh
- Listening to a song that's so good I have to walk round the block because I need to listen to it again before I get home
- Going home to find I actually made my bed for once and it looks really cosy and inviting
- Discovering a quiet corner of my office building that's not as busy
- Making someone laugh so much a little tear forms in the corner of their eye
- Laughing so much I'm not omitting any sounds just sort of doubling over slapping my thigh
- Sharing a problem with someone and feeling that bit of pressure lift off my chest
- Waking up and drinking in the smell of someone next to me who I love even though I'm very jealous they're still asleep
- Waking up in bed by myself and starfishing my heart out
- Looking at old family photographs and laughing at my old haircuts
- Randomly treating myself to a fancy shower gel or flowers or silky underpants
- Opening a fresh notebook and feeling like everything is possible
- Going to a big social event and finding that one person I happen to totally connect with

Maggy van Eijk

- Going to the pub after a long strenuous hike
- Getting drenched outside and diving straight into bed with a fresh set of PJs when I get home
- Also, getting into bed when you've put fresh sheets on
- Finding that perfect laundry detergent that makes everything smell like a meadow
- Making a salad that's both healthy and also miraculously sort of tastes OK
- And then eating a dessert after because I just had salad
- Spending a chunk of time with someone that I expect is about to end and then they suggest continuing on and staying out a bit longer
- Finding something totally random in a gift shop that I just have to get for someone
- Leaving myself enough time to get a fancy coffee before I get to my desk
- Also being the first one in so I get to revel in that calm before the storm
- Feeling a gentle ache in my muscles from doing something that didn't feel like exercise at all (e.g. helping someone move house or going for a bike ride or jumping into a pond)

The Skin

REMEMBER THiS WhEN YOU WaNT TO HUrT YOURSeLF

Sometimes my head gets so tangled up I resort to inflicting physical pain on myself in the hope of making some sense of it all. When I was sixteen, I self-harmed for the first time. It felt like I'd opened up a door that would never get shut again. I felt the brief endorphin rush as I broke my skin and red liquid trickled across my thigh. The rush was almost instantly replaced by fear. I felt extremely scared because I couldn't quite believe what I'd done. I crawled into bed and tried to make sense of the situation but my brain was zigzagging through my skull. I couldn't rationalise my actions.

Through my own fast and shallow breathing I could hear the soft voices of my parents in the living room.

My brain was caught up in a tennis match between two urges: go out there and ask for help, or stop crying, go to sleep and put a plaster on your arm (no one needs to know what you've done).

I wanted to choose the first option. I imagined what it would be like to walk into the living room and whisper 'Help.' My dad's eyes would widen the way they do when he's worried. My mum would lunge towards me and hug me. They'd get me a plaster and make me some tea. That part seemed easy. I could do that. Then came the tough bit. I would drink the tea and put my mug down. My dad would ask why I'm so upset. My mum would ask what happened to my arm and I knew that's when my throat would close up and block my voice from coming out. It seemed too painful, too awkward, too big of a task. Instead I shut my eyes, wrapped an old Euro Disney T-shirt around my wrist and went to sleep.

I often think about this moment. If only I'd nudged myself out of bed and into the living room. That moment became a pattern that repeated itself over and over. I have an urge to ask someone to help me – a counsellor, a boyfriend, a housemate or a friend – but instead I feel like I can't. This is my dirty secret and I should just get on with it. No one can help me, no one wants to help me.

Self-harm quickly became a crutch for me to manage the cacophony of negative voices whizzing around my head. In part because teenage me didn't know anxiety and depression were a thing. Self-harm helped me manage my symptoms, just in the worst way possible.

For me, self-harm feels like I'm standing on a bridge and the wind is so extreme it can blow me away at any moment, and then I find a little trapdoor that leads me down below, to another bridge where there's no wind and I can just move forward freely. Self-harm is that trapdoor.

Reasons why I've self-harmed in the past:

- I'm angry but the anger refuses to leave my body
- I'm struggling to be present, to be in my body and I need something to ground myself
- I'd rather be in physical pain than deal with emotional pain
- I'm desperately trying to find something that will zap me out of my zombie brain
- I'm upset about something but I can't quite put my finger on it and if I don't do something now it will swallow me whole
- I have disappointed myself so irreversibly I have to physically punish myself
- I have had too much to drink and it just seems like a completely logical thing to do
- I watched something on my laptop that triggered

a flashback to something I need to expel from
my brain

- I feel like my voice isn't being heard and it has
nowhere to go but scream angry red lines out onto
my body
- I've not self-harmed in years and I can finally be
in a place where I can get away with it because
there's no one watching over me and like a
naughty kid I give in to the urge
- I see all the scars that already sit on my arm and
it makes me sad and ashamed and hate myself and
so I think, 'Fuck it, what's one more going to do?'

Reasons I definitely haven't self-harmed, despite what
some people assume:

- I'm desperate for attention
- I've been listening to My Chemical Romance
all day
- I'm doing it out of spite
- I'm doing it to piss off my parents
- I'm weak
- I want people to feel sorry for me
- I'm showing off
- I'm addicted to the endorphins
- I'm being dramatic
- I'm overly sensitive

- I'm doing it to manipulate someone else
- I like blood
- I like creating problems for myself

I became extremely self-reliant on hurting myself, using many methods. Before going to sleep with my bloody arm wrapped in loo roll I'd set myself little reminders in the form of Post-it notes: 'Get help', 'Tell mum', 'Talk to SOMEONE!' Then morning would come and I'd gather these bits of paper in a hurry, embarrassed at how desperate they all sounded.

As a teenager, when self-harm scars became noticeable, my mum enforced a No Sharp Objects rule in my room. All the scissors, razors and tweezers were removed. This helped for a bit. Whilst it annoyed me I knew the inevitable confrontation that would arise if I protested would be far worse. Having my mum's beady eye scan over my limbs each morning felt intrusive but it did stop me harming for a few months, which felt long at the time.

Over the years, there's been only one other person who stopped my harming: P., my first boyfriend. The wounds that blossomed on my forearms upset him and the guilt I felt looking at his face each time he'd spot one outweighed any relief I was getting out of it. His life at this point wasn't exactly smooth sailing. He had a manic depressive parent he often had to track down in the middle of the night. I didn't want to be an addition to his escalating list of worries. I decided I'd stop. My intentions were good but once again I didn't stop harming for me, it was in someone else's interest. Slowly but surely I found other ways to get back into my habit.

At the age of twenty-six, my self-harm spiralled dangerously out of control. Between the first time I self-harmed at sixteen and then I'd seen six counsellors. I'd been on meds for five years. I'd stopped harming on and off for periods of time but I hadn't been able to quit full-time.

It was a lukewarm March evening. I was heartbroken and sad about how my life had derailed. Anything productive and helpful I'd learnt thanks to counselling and research I'd tossed aside. I was standing outside a pub in Stoke Newington with a lit cigarette in hand causing myself injuries that would require weekly visits to A&E for the next few months.

Inside were five friends; we were celebrating one of their birthdays. The evening was jolly. Someone I was getting to know better romantically was there too. Possibilities were in the air. Good things could have happened if I'd had less to drink, if I hadn't gone outside on my own, if I'd asked someone for help, if if if.

My life at this point was shrouded in the aftermath of yet another relationship coming to an end that meant I was constantly going back and forth between our old shared flat and my new room, loaded with boxes and crates and a torn-apart heart. And yet I had woken up that day feeling uncharacteristically optimistic. Today was the last trip I had to do and I felt relieved. This would mean the end of living in the in-between: I could finally start afresh. To make a celebratory morning out of it I treated myself to brunch in my old area: French toast with Greek yoghurt and peaches. I invited my friend who lived round the corner. I wanted him to celebrate with me. I felt proud that I'd reclaimed my old brunch spot. I could still enjoy things. Old things could feel new. I could do this.

Just as we'd placed our orders the universe decided to become a badly scripted romantic comedy: in walks my ex-boyfriend. I knew this by how drained of blood my friend's face had become. My ex hadn't walked in alone; he was there with a woman. Blonde, sequin top and a bright pink mini skirt.

My ex and his breakfast partner had their backs to us, so the most sensible option was to get through our breakfast (quickly), pay and then go (hopefully unnoticed). We ate our food in utter silence; like we were two kids playing hide-and-seek, wanting to remain hidden until an adult called us to safety. My friend let me walk out first and joined after. When we made it out into the fresh spring air we both exhaled a breath we'd been keeping in for half an hour.

A near hysterical laugh chimneyed up out of me and filled the empty street. I bent over to catch my breath; all this nervous energy was spilling out. I couldn't stop laughing. I tried to compose myself so we could keep walking. We walked to Clissold Park where we went round in circles dodging kids on tricycles. The grass was thick and heavy with spring. It was a beautiful day, which only seemed to mock the shit situation we'd just left behind. Despite all this I was still chuckling. I think it was easier to find the whole thing funny than admit how terrible it really felt. Instead, I focused on how unlikely it all was, how hilariously cruel the universe must be. My friend joined me in my laughter, albeit somewhat apprehensively. I then stopped and decided to voice the most superficial thought I was having underneath all that laughter: 'She's prettier than me, isn't she?' My friend assured me she wasn't, not that it mattered. We then began to tear her down in a way that's entirely unfair and cruel and it didn't make me feel better. I told my friend I was ready to go home, screw getting my things at my old flat. I needed to go back to bed.

'I'm not leaving you on your own.'

'No it's fine, I'll be OK.'

'Still. I'm not leaving you.'

On his insistence, we ventured into my new neighbourhood and watched a Ryan Gosling film at the local Picturehouse cinema. The handsome lead was getting the girl, the bad guys were getting shot and all I could think about was how utterly pointless relationships were for me. My three years with my ex weren't as meaningful as I'd thought. Within the space of a few days our history had been reduced to an empty flat with tragic bits of Blu-Tack in the place where photos once lived. He'd already moved on. He was bringing women home. I was completely replaceable.

After wasting fifteen pounds on a ticket for a film I was paying zero attention to I decided to push my dark thoughts away. You know in a cartoon when a character has a nightmare and they shake their head, dispelling the nightmare from their body? That's what I was doing. I kept thinking, 'Just get to the end of the day. There's a party in a pub. You can drink then. Just get to the pub. You'll be fine.'

At the pub I played the part of 'happy friend'. I smiled, I laughed on cue and I sat up straight with my hands neatly folded in my lap like a bunch of flowers. My movements were so precise, so calculated, that they were tell-tale signs that things weren't really OK.

I stopped talking to anyone. I was no longer contributing my own bits of conversation. I was nodding along, feigning attention. I always find that if you nod and narrow your eyes ever so slightly people are under the impression you're listening to them. I didn't want to listen. I didn't want to be there. My brain had made its decision for me. I wanted to stop hurting so I needed to go out and hurt myself.

'Off for a smoke,' I announced.

'Fancy some company out there?'

'No, I'll be fine. Be right back.'

Once outside I lit my cigarette and I knew immediately I wasn't going to smoke it. I'd wanted to cut myself all day but under the watchful eye of my friend I'd been unable to. I didn't have anything sharp in my wallet – I must have thrown out my 'tools' the last time I promised myself I'd stop harming. At this point my brain was like an overpacked suitcase about to burst. I needed an outlet; I needed some relief. All I had was my cigarette.

I walked over to a big black bin and stood behind it. I was hidden away from a table full of smokers. I felt like an addict about to take a hit. I could get away with harming if I stayed here. No one would try to stop me.

There was too much wine in my system for me to put my self-harm urge on hold. Desolate heartbreak had anchored itself in. I held the cigarette to my skin. I felt a dull ache in my forearm but it wasn't enough. I moved the cigarette up my arm and dug it in deeper, longer. I stared out at the cars whizzing past me. This wasn't enough, I needed more. I did it again and again until my cigarette finished.

I put my cardigan on and walked back inside the pub on autopilot. I did feel better, sort of. I felt powerful and in control. I felt like I'd done the one thing I'd wanted to do all day: I had punished myself and it felt good. After a few more sips of wine I thought: 'All right, round one complete, off for more.' I repeated the process again. I left the cigarette on my skin even longer. Vicious thoughts entered my head like a drill bit. They were overpowering. They told me I deserved this. They told me I'd ruined a perfectly good relationship. They told me it was no wonder he'd moved on already considering how much of a shitbag girlfriend I was. I melted myself down with cruel, judgemental thoughts and slid what was left of me into the cracks in the pavement. My cigarette was done. I went back inside the pub, finished my wine and thought about going outside again. Only, I'd used my last cigarette, I didn't have any more.

'Are you OK?' my friend asked.

My head nodded a confident yes but from inside a tiny voice crawled out of my mouth. A voice that was scared and afraid and knew what I'd been doing wasn't OK. My throat opened up just a tiny bit, just enough to let one word out: 'Help.'

I stayed the night at my friend's house and left a trail of blood and pus on his white sheets. My arm looked like anti-drug propaganda: Watch What Happens When You Shoot Heroin into Your Arm.

I took myself to A&E the next day. My arm was covered in seeping wounds that were starting to yellow. I went up to the reception desk and whispered something about burn wounds and they told me to take a seat. I looked around at the other patients and tried to play a game of: Guess Why They're Here. There was a twisted ankle, perhaps a kidney infection and someone who had something stuck in their eye. When it was my turn to be seen I'd completely forgotten the speech I'd written for myself about how I'd gotten these injuries. The excuses had fallen away.

'Did someone do these to you?'

'No.'

'How did you get them?'

'I did them to myself.'

'All right, let's take a proper look.'

Whilst the nurse attended my arms I sent myself into a guilt spin: 'Look at all those hospital resources they're wasting on you, not to mention the nurse's time – everyone knows how understaffed the NHS is! You're a burden to society!'

My guilt trip came to a sudden halt thanks to a sharp pain in my arm that shot down to my wrist. The triage nurse was trying to establish whether I'd burnt my nerves. Bits of my wound seemed to be devoid of feeling but the parts that weren't hurt like hell. My nerves were fine thanks.

Eventually she wrapped my arm up like a really shit Christmas present and gave me a bandage sleeve to cover my entire arm. She handed me a list of cleaning instructions and I had to promise I'd come back three times a week for the next couple of weeks so they could dress the wounds. I followed her rules diligently. For someone who showered about three times a week at a stretch and lived off tins of sweetcorn and salt and vinegar Pringles I was determined to do this the right way. I followed her rules and treated my body like a friend who needed help rather than my enemy.

Despite my best intentions, when I came back to the same nurse on my third week she didn't look pleased. The wounds had refused to heal. Fluid was still leaking out everywhere. I was referred to a burns clinic in a hospital in Chelsea and the nurse hoped the specialists would know what to do.

When I walked through the bright white big streets of south London I felt so alien amongst the beautiful rows of houses. I shuffled past Instagrammable coffee shops and young mothers juggling chubby babies and yoga mats. I decided I'd have one cigarette on my way there and one on the way back to reward myself. The irony of smoking whilst my arm was covered in third-degree burns felt like a secret rebellion. The fuckers weren't healing anyway.

The hospital itself was massive and overwhelming. It

smelt of antiseptic cleansers. The bright light bounced off the white tiles into my eyes. Plastic flowers dotted the walls and guided me to an empty reception desk. This felt like a good excuse to leave as no one was there to tell me where to go, until a big green sign ruined my chance of escape. I followed the arrows pointing to the Burns Unit. In my head I imagined this big smokey furnace where people would be crawling round the floor, their skin crispy and charred. Obviously, it's nothing like that at all. The unit was sterile and clinical. Everyone in the waiting room was like me: upright, but with some part of their body wrapped in gauze.

I was ushered into a room by an Irish lady who looked so huggable I wanted to disappear into her soft arms. She sat me down and began inspecting my wounds. 'How did you do these?' When I told her what had happened I added a meek 'sorry' at the end. She told me I didn't have to apologise: 'My daughter does that.' I didn't know if she meant the self-harm or the apologising but I nodded like I'd known her daughter for years.

The room filled up with more nurses. They each inspected my arm and poked the wounds. I felt my stomach lurch, my sight became blotchy and I forced my focus onto their chatter to stifle the panic that was rising inside my body. The nurses were teasing each other about who put the most sugar in their tea. I focused on the words, the sound of their laughter. I pretended I was at the hairdresser getting lost in the chatter of friendly women having their hair done. As they nattered away and rustled their plastic aprons I christened these women my three fairy godmothers. But instead of getting me ready for the ball, they were patching me up to go out there and face the real world again.

Being in that hospital room, handing over my broken body to other people, made me realise it was the first time I'd let other people take care of me. They were scrubbing me clean, tearing bits of scabs and dead skin off and filling the holes in my arm with antiseptic and honey. They made me promise I'd come back the following week.

I wish I could say that night outside the pub was my final harming episode. It wasn't. Self-harm has been my coping mechanism for over ten years. It's as natural to me as sneezing or brushing my teeth. I've normalised it in my head so when I feel the need I just do it: 'Why not? What's the big deal?' What I have learnt is that it is a big deal because my body deserves better. The lattice-work of scars on my skin tells me I hate my body, I don't respect it, it's a warzone. Self-love is a term everyone throws around like it's fluffy and easy but to go through something and accept it rather than work it out on the battlefield of your body is actually one of the hardest things to do.

73

Things you could do instead of self-harm:

- Tell someone near you that you need them to distract you – you don't have to tell them why. I once made my friend, a diehard Bon Jovi fan, list all his favourite Bon Jovi songs in order. I closed my eyes and submerged myself in his enthusiasm and the words of each title. It worked (thanks Bon Jovi!)

- Get a pen and a scrap piece of paper and scribble as hard and fast as you can

- Type out your thoughts on your phone. Don't stop typing until you've let it all out (I have a dozen notes on my iPhone that just say FUCKUFKCUFKCUFCK over and over again)

- Buy a pot of slime from a toy shop and roll and stretch and poke the goo between your fingers

- Bake something that requires paying close attention to step-by-step instructions

- Get up and run, really fast. Don't stop until your heart is leaping up to your throat

- Scream into a pillow (sometimes I make a pillow sandwich with two pillows and my own head in the middle)

- Have a warm shower and shock your system with a sudden rush of cold water

- Put on your favourite music from when you were

a teen and sing along really, really loudly (any Fall Out Boy song does the trick for me)

- Find a dog, any dog, and pet it
- Dye your hair
- Cut your toenails
- Pop three big pieces of bubblegum in your mouth
- Blow up a balloon and then pop it
- Reorganise your wardrobe
- Watch a film you can pretty much quote along to: *Superbad* does it for me
- Doodle your dream house
- Download *The Sims*
- Sign yourself up for a bunch of exercise classes in the near future
- Rub an ice cube over your wrist
- Paint a delicate flower on your skin
- Follow a bunch of tattoo artists on Instagram and rank your favourite pieces
- Organise your bookcase by colour
- Come up with a new signature in case you become world-famous
- Make a playlist for someone
- Phone a friend
- Do a beauty tutorial on YouTube

- Bang your hands loudly on a piano
- Or actually play the piano if you can
- Watch a shark documentary
- Record yourself voicing all your anger, but do it in Snapchat so you can add a funny filter and make your voice sound like a cute raccoon

Most self-harmers can recall a time someone said something awful about their scars. Special shout-out to the man who stopped in his tracks to yell: 'Fucking hell! Did you fall into a cactus!' at me. Or that guy from uni who went for: 'Woah, were you mauled by a tiger?' Those are the kinds of reactions that make you want to stay inside and wrap your whole body in a massive plaster for the rest of your life.

One morning I was on my way to work, breathing in the stale air of an underground Tube carriage in summer. It was rush hour and my body was being squished into someone else's. I reached up to grab the railing above me and I could see the woman beside me staring at my arm. I wanted her eyes to stop zigzagging over my body. I felt trapped in my own skin. I wasn't just a woman on a train getting to work; I was a walking billboard for my own depression. I felt naked and unsafe, as if I'd just screamed: 'WELCOME TO THE TRAIN EVERYONE, I'M YOUR CO-PASSENGER AND I CUT MYSELF SOMETIMES.' Getting off that train was like plunging into cold sea on a scorching hot day. I rubbed my hand over my forearm as if to wipe away my scars and headed into work.

When I see self-harm scars on other people, a sequence of reactions happens to me. First, there's physical sensation: dizziness, nausea, all the usual anxiety ailments. It feels like I'm being confronted with something I didn't ask for; someone else's pain reminding me of my own: 'You do this too, you know? Remember all those times you filled the sink with your blood? Remember those times you went too far?' Then there's the overwhelming worry for that person: 'God, I hope they're OK,' combined with an invisible link that binds us together. We're two people out in the world doing things we're expected to do – like going to school or work, doing some shopping, eating in a restaurant – but we've both clearly, in private, succumbed to this horribly destructive act. Should we exchange numbers? Should we hug? Should we run away from each other?

I'm always fascinated by other people's scars that aren't self-inflicted; I love hearing the stories and the tales that surround battle wounds. Scars are a record of someone's journey thus far. They're souvenirs your body insists on clinging onto. I've tried to see my own scars this way. Just because the stories are sad doesn't mean I have to dismiss them. My scars are a testament to the fact that I somehow made it out the other end time and time again.

I don't worry about covering up scars. On a bad day

I see them as angry red rosettes, awarded to me for having achieved the highest level of fucking up. On a good day however, I see them as a testament to my survival. I interviewed Ruby Wax for BuzzFeed about her book *Frazzled*. I told her how all her mental health campaigning had meant a lot to me and she asked if it was OK to know what kind of mental health problems I'd experienced. I told her my story, and she looked at my arms and said: 'You're very brave for not covering up.' After the interview I walked around Kensington Gardens and for the first time I felt that maybe I am a bit brave.

> 'I DO IT SO IT FEELS LIKE HELL'
> — Sylvia Plath, *Lady Lazarus*

There are myriad ways you can hurt yourself. It's not always as visible as cigarette burns or cuts and bruises. Self-poisoning is on the rise amongst teenagers. It's a very tricky form of self-harm for parents and friends to pick up on because there are no visible scars. Self-poisoning tends to involve using alcohol, food, painkillers or illegal drugs to test the limits of damage you can cause to your body.

As with most self-harm, it's not necessarily about suicide. When I self-poisoned I never wanted to die but it seemed like the only way to match the anger and isolation that consumed me. The pain I felt in my stomach after ingesting a stupid amount of paracetamol felt like a secret I kept with myself, deep down in my belly. 'This pain is yours,' it said, 'it's no one else's.'

I did the same with drinking. Teenage exploration with alcohol isn't always as dramatic as self-poisoning, but drinking with the intent of doing damage is far more serious. It's no longer about curiosity. For me, it was born out of self-loathing and the hope of finding some release. You're probably not using alcohol to self-harm when you're drinking in the park with your friends on a Friday night. You do it when you get up at 7am, before your parents go to work, adding an obscene amount of whiskey to your cola. You do it when you're hiding cans of beers under your bed to drink through the night. You do it when you mix all the alcohol you can find in the kitchen in a bottle, shake it, and genuinely believe that by the time you finish the whole bottle things will feel better. Instead, you vomit and you go to bed feeling nauseous and drowsy and gross.

My teenage binge drinking ironically subsided as soon as it was legal for me to drink. When I went to uni and I could technically drink myself into blackout oblivion I stayed away from alcohol. As a student, alcohol became associated with being social, having friends and having fun. I had neither of those things and I feared alcohol because it seemed to represent a life I wouldn't be able to have. Plagued with panic attacks I was so scared of my own brain that I didn't want to experiment with drugs either. I was barely keeping it together sober, what would my brain do to me if I added more chemicals to it?

After uni, things changed between alcohol and me. That side of me that existed as a teenager returned. I wanted wine to comfort me, beer to get me through a tough day and shots to drown out whatever it was I was worrying about at the time.

I wanted alcohol to submerge me completely, to turn off the lights. I wanted alcohol to make me cooler, more interesting. I wanted alcohol to replace the parts of me I hated with a more fun, sociable version of myself. Sometimes this worked – I evolved into a chattier, dancier version of me. Sometimes it did the opposite – I became even more down, even harder on myself.

A letter to Sauvignon Blanc

Dear Sauv,

Can I call you Sauv? I think yes. I mean, we've known each other long enough.

On that note, I know I need to see you less. Don't roll your eyes. I know I've said this many times before but I'm serious.

Do you remember when we first met? I was twelve, finding out which form of self-destruction would fit best. I was testing the limits of my body; Sometimes I'd bang my head against a wall until it bled. Sometimes I'd etch angry red lines into my thighs with safety pins. Sometimes I'd eat a jar of peanut butter and puke it back up. And then I met you. You were another way to test myself. I used to sneak you into water bottles and pretend you were apple juice. I'd drink you until my stomach felt a pang and then I'd stop, close my eyes and blink the dizziness away.

The first time I got drunk wasn't in a park with friends. There wasn't a boy I fancied. I didn't impress anyone. Instead, I was alone in bed, clutching my belly, trying to read a book whilst the blurry words bled into the illustrations. When my mum's friend came to check on me one afternoon I thought, 'Shit, I'm busted.' Then I had a brilliant idea. 'It's my period,' I groaned. She left the room and came back with a hot water bottle and stroked my head. It would be four years before I'd get my first period. I felt pretty smart.

Sauv, I wish I'd spent a little less time with you growing up — twelve was too young. All those stomach aches were futile, they never warned me away from you. You have this eerie ability to slow everything down. It's wonderful but it's haunting. You're a depressant. You mess up my already muddied levels of serotonin. You confuse cells — those well-meaning cells that take care of mood, desire and appetite. In your hands they get swirled around

*like a frustrated painter messing up his pallet. You mix
everything into a shade of blackout grey.*

*I don't mean to say you always make me feel sad.
Sometimes you make me feel invincible, sexy. You also
bring me comfort, a dilatory calm. Coming home after a
shit day you rejig my thoughts. When I'm cold and dizzy
from Oxford Street's congested pavements you warm
me up. You make loneliness appealing. You joggle me
out of the numbness of everyday existence. You make me
feel, even if those feelings are slightly skewed. You crawl
into my blood, wrap your spindly fingers around my
thoughts and, without warning, yank them right out of
me. 'Go over there! Go do that! Go feel that! Go exist!'
I can hear you roar into the echo chamber. Sometimes
you sound like a cheerleader who just snorted her best
friend's Ritalin.*

*The first glass of you always feels like magic. The
second feels more settled, more familiar, and the third is
almost automatic, a routine. I'm not even excited about it.
I approach the barman like I'm approaching my husband
in a marriage that's gone past its expiry date. We're
both there to perform a task. We know what we want; we
exchange goods, rinse and repeat.*

*I talk a big game when I'm drunk, but one I always
find myself apologising for. I've had to say sorry for
kissing somebody else's boyfriend, for punching a
man who was just trying to get me home safe and for*

*vomiting in my own mouth so I
wouldn't ruin the taxi driver's
car (this plan was going great
until I sneezed).*

*I've consumed you in a melancholy,
quiet way too. That night I was maid of
honour, I smiled away the feeling that
I'd never be good enough to be part of this wedding, took
a sip of you and picked at the Mr & Mrs Merlot label,
collecting a little confetti heap beneath my hands.*

*What I mean to say with all of this is that I want to
break up with you, Sauv, just for a little bit. Don't take
it the wrong way. I'm sure we'll see each other soon. I just
need a bit of space. My brain needs some space.*

Love,

Maggy

The problem with alcohol is that it stuffs my head with
lies. It makes me lose sight of where I am and what I'm
doing. With alcohol in my blood, I say yes to anything. I'll
wander anywhere. I lose track of what's dangerous and
what isn't. On top of that, my medication means it can
be dangerous to add alcohol to my system as I'm prone
to blacking out. It's a strange type of unconsciousness
where my body is still moving but my mind is completely
shut. I'll wake up the next day to thousands of Facebook

messages I fired off in my drunken haze, or I'll find myself in a strange room with a flurry of bruises dotted around my ribs.

Alcohol seems like a comforting friend, but alcohol doesn't tell you the truth.

Alcohol tells me I'm invincible.

Alcohol transforms every person in the bar into a vessel for me to escape in.

Alcohol tells me that it's OK to hurt myself.

Alcohol tells me that it feels good to hurt myself.

Alcohol tells me I need more

drugs

sex

everything.

Alcohol tells me no one really loves me.

Alcohol tells me I'm going to die soon.

Alcohol tells me the only thing I have to offer is my body.

Alcohol tells me my life is a badly scripted film someone else has written.

Alcohol tells me the only way out is pain.

Alcohol tells me the only way out is the darkness of a blackout.

The Gut

5

REMEMBER THiS
WhEN YOU CaN'T STaND
YOUR OWn BODY

I have waged a constant battle with my own shape. I've often seen my body as flabby, shapeless, a bit blob-like. What seemed to instigate my attitude towards my body was the very late arrival of puberty that descended upon me like an unwanted guest. I didn't get a period until I was seventeen and it felt like not only was my uterus spitting out blood, but volcanoes erupted on my chest overnight. My flat butt developed into two big pillowy mounds. There was hair everywhere and the tufts under my pits carried a sour odour with them. A foreign entity was taking over my body. I was being pushed out, evicted. It was saying: this isn't yours anymore, this belongs to someone else.

I'd squeeze and pinch and poke my own flesh. I wanted to fight back. I dreamed of getting a knife and slicing off my new lumps and curves. I'd sit in the bath and lean to one side, clutching all the flesh that collected. Why couldn't I just remove it? Why was it there? What had I done?

I found it was much harder to hide in my new body. Men stared harder and longer. I walked with my arms across my chest to stop by breasts from bouncing. I tucked my butt in when I was walking so it wouldn't invite anyone to touch it.

I experimented with different clothing styles to try and reclaim my identity that my breasts had taken away from me. I wasn't curvy and feminine, that just didn't suit me. Instead I tried to go for punk. I had rainbow dreadlocks and safety pins in my ears. I embodied a surfer girl aesthetic for a year even though I'd never stood on a surfboard. In uni I mainly wore my boyfriend's clothes. I liked how baggy his T-shirts were. Sometimes I'd wear his large old man's boxer shorts underneath a dress. I liked how unsexy they made me feel, but safe at the same time. Femininity with a secret layer of manliness.

When these unwanted changes made me feel out of control I sought comfort in food. Food was my friend, enemy and refuge. I began bingeing on bags of Doritos, pastries and loaves of bread whilst telling my body: 'Fuck you, I control you, I can do what I want.' But the full, sickly feeling didn't feel like rebellion, it made me feel even more gross and horrible. I began purging after a binge. I bought laxatives. I made my stomach feel sick from chugging litres of water after I ate an entire cake.

Sometimes I'd stay home from school because it was easier to avoid food that way. Then I'd freak out that I wasn't getting any exercise because going to school meant a half-hour bike ride so instead I'd run up and down the stairs. I'd feel so hungry it felt like my insides were eating themselves and then I'd run to the kitchen and devour whatever I could find.

I needed discipline and I needed a sense of routine so I counted calories in everything. I'd make lists and meal plans and exercise goals and weight goals. I set arbitrary challenges for myself like:

TUESDAY: Eat nothing but grapes.

WEDNESDAY: Only eat green food.

Food was violently stripped of its simplicity and was given a new outfit: one of obsession, compulsion and punishment.

I wasn't able to look at food differently until my early twenties. This was thanks to therapy, which helped me accept some of the things that are out of my control. However, initially I had my own tactic: don't think about food at all.

I developed this surface-level blasé attitude about what

I ate: 'Oh, whatever, I'm just going to drink two pints of milk and eat a loaf of bread and devour this cupcake right here – who the fuck cares?' For me, caring about what I consumed felt triggering. It would set off a fear that I'd go back to my old ways. Food would become too powerful. I'd lose myself in its hold over me. I'd be the hungry marionette with food controlling the strings. The only thing I could do was convince myself that I was beyond caring. Problem is: food is everywhere, and food triggers are everywhere.

After I worked in a theatre I got my first proper London job working for a student offers and deals website. I sat at a table with women who had collectively decided to do a healthy eating challenge. What gave their plan a sinister turn for me was that they announced whoever lost the most weight by Christmas won. The winner received money they had pooled together and a pair of yoga leggings.

I stopped munching on my peanut butter and sugar sandwich (FYI, when money's tight, peanut butter and sugar is the most delicious sandwich spread). I could feel a little well of anger bubble up in my stomach. I walked away from my table and did what I usually did when something frustrated me: I marched around the building. A friend caught up with me and I explained what I'd witnessed, only it came out more dramatic than I intended: 'They are bad women!' I yelled. 'They are bad for each other. They are being bad women. I hate them so much!'

A few years later at a different job, I had a similar episode where I actually got so mad I marched to HR after I heard a group of co-workers openly assess how many calories were in each sandwich we'd been given as a free lunch that day. It was becoming a strange ritual for that particular group. Free food would arrive and they'd stand in front of it counting calories like they were evaluating antiques at an auction. Reporting them turned me into a schoolgirl nark but I couldn't help my reaction. On the surface I was angry but beneath that I was frightened. I didn't want anything to send me back to teenage me who could look at any item of food (or even a teaspoon of semen) and tell you exactly how many calories it contained.

I wish there was a way to strip away from food all the other add-ons: the shame, the control, the power. How can food ever just be food? How can you look at pizza and just see it as pizza and nothing else?

Something that's nudged me in the right direction is finding pride in what I'm putting into my mouth (that's what she said). I started cooking more. I'm not a great chef – in fact, the second I started showing off my slow-cooker lasagna on Instagram I lost a ton of followers, but that's just by the by. Eating something I put together myself makes it easier for me to see it as what it is: nutrients, ingredients, sauce, a recipe, etc. The stuff I make is rarely super-healthy but it's always better than ordering pizza or falling asleep with Doritos dust on my forehead.

When looking for recipes online, the middle ground of good hearty, healthy food is often hard to find. It tends to be either super-indulgent chocolate and banana pancake deep-fried in butter all wrapped around a Mars Bar *or* a bowl of kale with two grains of salt. It's easy to steer clear of the indulgent stuff because frankly I'm not that good a baker. The sad bowls of kale are harder to avoid. They're everywhere. Sad bowls of kale are an epidemic.

We've been hit by a white lady wellness wave: there are cookbooks, Instagram accounts, YouTube series all about assembling chia bowls and milking almonds and predominantly these come from white women with topknots and T-shirt that say 'Shanti Sundays'. This is not a sweeping statement – just log onto Instagram.

A lot of the language these authors use centres around the phrase 'clean eating'. Clean eating basically means trying to eat as many whole foods as possible – so foods that aren't processed, refined or handled. In short: foods that are as close to their natural form as they can be. There's nothing wrong with that if that's the kind of food that tickles your pickle (and you're making sure you're getting enough nutrients). The problem lies with the phrase 'clean eating', implying that all other foods that don't meet this criteria are 'dirty'. Culinary queen Nigella Lawson nailed it when she was speaking on *Woman's Hour* in 2015 and said: 'I think that food should not be used as a way of persecuting oneself and I think really one should look to get pleasure about what's good rather than either think, "Oh no, that's dirty, bad or sinful", or "eating is virtuous".'

Nigella became my food idol for many reasons. Her cooking shows are dazzlingly pornographic. For starters, she's the most beautiful being that has ever graced this planet, which makes watching her an incredibly sexy experience, but there's also something so joyful in the way in which she prepares her food and how she eats it when she's done. I particularly remember a shot of her in silk pyjamas going down to her fridge at midnight to eat one of her leftover cheese soufflés. There was no shame or secrecy, the woman just fancied a fucking soufflé. It's hers. She can have it. No big deal.

Nigella taught me to love cooking for other people. To share what you've made and bask in the glow of compliments about your food (even if your pie is undercooked and people are pretty much chomping on raw dough). She taught me how to relax when you make food and how it can be meditative. Stirring risotto for an hour whilst putting on Whitney Houston's *Greatest Hits* in the background is one of the most wonderful feelings in the world.

I can't find this kind of joy in clean eating, or any other diets for that matter. When I purchased a few of the apps that belong to some of these clean eating ambassadors it struck me how restrictive they are, and not to mention expensive. I was running to Whole Foods in my lunch break to get spices and powder and shakes of things I still can't pronounce. I wanted to be as happy as the girl doing a headstand, drinking my home-brewed kombucha, but my depression, lack of money, stress and inability to even do a headstand were all getting in the way. I was blaming myself for not being able to attain the lifestyle I was seeing prescribed to me. I couldn't keep up.

Food fads are rife and the science around food is incredibly conflicting. One day a headline will tell you blueberries might cure your bipolar disorder but the next day blueberries give you terrible acne. Reading these headlines and studies I found myself yet again feeling like I couldn't keep up. So I stopped. I stopped trying to impose rules other people have created (often without proper research) on my own life. Articles where a blonde lady tells me gluten is 'toxic' will go straight in the bin. As will a podcast I listened to not that long ago about hormones in food driving women clinically insane. After listening I got so paranoid I started tearing down my shower curtain (apparently there are hormones in shower curtains – WHO KNEW?). Thank god I have my trusty friend Kelly, a science editor at BuzzFeed, who will tell me that it's safe to keep my shower curtains up, gluten won't kill me and blueberries won't make my mental health any worse.

Striking a good relationship with food has been hard work. What you eat and how it makes you feel can be such a minefield, and figuring it all out is still very much a work in progress, but here are some things I have learnt along the way:

- I try to pay attention to what I'm eating and limit the times I eat mindlessly whilst watching repeats of *The Office* on my laptop. I pay close attention to the taste and texture of what I'm chewing on and even when I'm hungry as hell I try not to wolf anything down
- I've started to tell myself I actually deserve good food. I deserve to feel healthy. I deserve to roast vegetables and eat spicy peach and smashed avocado. I deserve to spend money on fresh ingredients. I deserve to wake up feeling like I can handle the day instead of being weighed down by what I ate the night before

◉ Greengrocers are a godsend. I sadly moved
away from the best greengrocer in London on
Newington Green, but I used to cram my basket
full of fresh ingredients and walk out having only
spent a fiver. It changed how I thought about food
and what I considered to be a good meal. I now
wanted at least three different kinds of veg with
everything I was making. I wanted to use spices
and sea salt and coconut oil. When you only pop
down to your corner shop or your Tesco Express
you forget that you can walk a little further
and probably find vegetables and fruit that are
fresher and cheaper

◉ Don't compare what's on your plate to what's
on someone else's. Just because your friend is
eating a salad doesn't mean you have to as well.
Similarly, if everyone else is tucking into steak
and spare ribs but you really fancy something
smaller go for it

◉ I try not to use food to manage my emotions but
it's a process. The more I tell myself not to stress-
eat the more I end up doing it. So I have tried to
change the foods I do still stress-eat – instead of
eating raw cake batter I'll try almonds or apricots
or rice cakes covered in chocolate

◉ I try not to buy my drug foods. There are certain
foods that when I have them in my house I eat

them in one go. I have to. They're too dangerous for me, even talking about them makes me twitch. French Fancies will be consumed within ten minutes and not just one, nope, it'll be the whole box. Same with ketchup flavoured crisps, jars of peanut butter and apple pie. I once threw away half an apple pie so I wouldn't eat the entire thing only to dig it out of the bin and eat it with my hands. Classy

My body and I have been on a long journey together. I'm trying to recognise it as a place I live in. A place that gives me a home. I spent years draping towels and sheets over mirrors in my house so I wouldn't have to be confronted with the monstrosity I considered my body to be. I don't do that any more. I try and look at myself properly at least once a week. Full frontal nudity: straight into the mirror. I try to say a couple things about what I'm seeing. It can't be anything negative, but it doesn't have to be overtly positive either. I usually start with: 'I have a mole on my butt', 'My right nipple goes into hiding' or 'My thighs are stuck together' — on a good day I might add, 'and that's pretty cute'.

HOW TO BE NICE TO YOUR BODY

One word: dance. Dance for so long you literally forget what it's like to feel self-conscious. Dance in the dark, in your chair, dance whilst lying down in bed. Close your eyes and move your body the way you feel like. No one's watching, do whatever weird movement comes into your head.

Have a really fucking luxurious bath. Put Drake on in the background. Add rose petals to the water. Get as many bubbles as you can handle. Touch your body, all over. You don't have to feel anything, you don't have to shout 'I LOVE MY LADY LUMPS' from the rooftops, just acknowledge that you have a body, that it's yours and that you're grateful for it.

Your body isn't made of problem zones. There are no bad patches or gross bits. See your body as a whole. It's not a cage, it's a canvas. It's not a prison, it's a spaceship that will take you wherever you want to go.

Decorate your body the way you want to. I like tattoos and cheap supermarket hair dye. Maybe you want a nipple piercing or a shaved head or maybe a fringe is radical enough for you.

Don't respond to people who don't treat your body with respect. Don't respond to people who misgender you. Don't respond to people who ignore you.

Treat your body like a garden; you need water to grow your hair, you need sunlight and attention. You need nourishing. You can't punish a garden and expect it to grow. You can't chop it up, tear bits out, slice off branches and expect it to bloom.

Appreciate all the things your body can do and don't berate it for the things it can't.

Fill your social feeds, your scrapbook, your saved images with people you admire. People who look similar to you and people who say 'Fuck you' to beauty standards and hold themselves defiantly.

Remember that women often get made to feel like their body is an enemy. That men use our bodies, transfer their desires onto our skin and give us no choice but to go with it. When I was growing up, I blamed my big ass for street harassment and catcalling. I blamed my breasts for all the times teachers looked down my top and made me feel uncomfortable. I blamed my long legs for when my skirt rode up and someone sitting down on the train tried to peer up it. My body made me feel disgusting; it was a magnet for unwanted attention. But my body never deserved that loathing – other people who are unable to respect the female body are the ones to blame.

Remember that your body is a miracle machine: your skin replaces itself once a month, you have 62,000 miles worth of veins and you create 180 million red blood cells every hour. In short: Your body is a badass. It deserves your respect and admiration.

Look at yourself in the mirror. I find it hard and I find myself almost always unable to not pull a 'gross' face but I try not to. Look at it. Notice what your body looks like – where it curves, where it shapes, where there are scars, where there are bumps. The more I look at my own body the more I'm aware of what's there and it's easier for me to accept this is the body I'm in and this is the best body for me. When I ignore my body or pretend it isn't there I don't feel like it's ever truly mine.

Hug yourself, fondle your breasts, stroke your pubes. Say 'You're the best' or 'You rock', or whatever it is you'd like someone to say to you, say it to your body.

The Heart

REMEMBER THiS
WhEN YOU'RE FALLiNG
In LOVE

Now you've assembled even just a small dose of self-love you're in the right shape to get out there and date your socks off. Dating is always nerve-wracking but dating with anxiety feels like you're taking a wailing baby with you wherever you go. Yes, this restaurant is nice but there's a screaming toddler on my lap. How am I supposed to give off a good impression when I'm trying to keep a tidal wave of panic from rising out of my stomach? I want to come across Michelle Pfeiffer-esque (specifically Pfeiffer circa *Grease 2*) but I feel a lot more like that girl from *The Exorcist*. Messy, possessed and devilishly horny.

To me, dating has always felt like a job interview or a trial shift. You're trying to figure out if you're a good fit. You have to be your best, most interesting, impressive self whilst trying to find out as much about the other person as possible. I give myself credit for being quite good at asking questions. I'm inquisitive and genuinely find most people interesting, but I have to make sure I don't veer into full-on interrogating them.

When the questions get flipped the other way round and I'm on the receiving end I struggle. I freeze and try to scrape the barrel of my brain for an interesting fact about myself but I come up empty. I want to tell the person about how my shoulders are double-jointed but instead I mumble something like 'shuh du juh' which is met by even more panic so I compensate by barfing up an endless stream of random and often inappropriate facts about myself, from what I ate that day to what my cup size is, and that sometimes my OCD is so bad I have to repeat everything you say under my breath three times.

For all the anxiety dating has caused me I've never sworn off dating full stop. Whenever I've been single I've thrown myself into a flurry of dates to keep trying out new strategies until some sort of action plan sticks. I'd carry with me a repertoire of stories I considered to be interesting so my brain freeze wouldn't be so detrimental.

My go-to I'm-on-a-date-and-there's-silence story has

always been this random fact about Singapore airport. I actually have no idea if this is true or not but apparently if your flight is delayed for more than five hours you get a free tour of the city *and* you get to use their pool for free. (If you work at Singapore airport and you know this is in fact a lie please can you inform the dozens of guys in London who I've told this to?) I'd use this story or any of my probably false airport facts as a starting point to ease my nerves (did you know that in 1987 American Airlines saved $40,000 by removing one olive from each salad served in first class?).

The only problem is I relied so much on my airport facts that I'd start to lose track of who I'd used them on and who I hadn't. On date two I'd whip out my fact about Sydney to Dallas being the longest flight in distance and realise I'd already used that one on the first date or maybe even just an hour earlier. Slowly, my handy tool became my worst enemy. I sounded like a glitchy Furby spewing our airport facts until I ran out of batteries.

So how did I learn to chill out? In short: I didn't. The biggest thing I learnt is that I'm always going to be stressed. There will be dates where I'm not *as* stressed and this is a lot to do with the person I'm with. It's the little things people do that make anxious daters feel at ease. For some reason when my date actually uses my name (e.g., 'Nice to meet you, Maggy' or 'Maggy, where did you grow up?') it feels like they think I'm important and worthy of their time. When someone is friendly to the waiter I feel like they're polite and I can trust them. When they're all right drinking but not constantly rushing to the bar to get another round I feel like we can have a good time without getting wrecked.

There are a few things I can do myself to feel more comfortable. Firstly: recruit help from elsewhere. When I'm walking to wherever I'm meeting my date I like to be on the phone to a friend. Someone who won't mind that I suddenly hang up when I spot my date and someone who won't mind my running commentary as I'm looking for the venue: 'I'm walking down the street. I can see the bar. I can see myself in the reflection of this window. I look like a gremlin. It's fine. Gremlins are kind of sexy in a scary way. My date might totally be into that. OK, I'm walking past the bar so they don't see me standing there waiting like I have nothing better to do. I'm walking. OMG I CAN SEE THEM. FUCK. OK. SHIT. Should I wave? No. No I won't wave. I'll be OK. OK. GOTTA GO THEY'VE SPOTTED ME BYE!'

Once I'm on my date I need to have quick access to water. Water eases my anxiety. Without water I panic that I might get dehydrated and shrivel like a prune on the spot. I also get paranoid about choking on food on a date. When my whole body is riddled with nerves the simple act of swallowing a bit of veggie burger demands all my attention. I need water to help move things down.

I once went on a Tinder date to Brick Lane where we bought some Ethiopian curries that we ate sat outside on a park bench. The food was amazing but I felt a tiny twinge in my tummy. It was probably just a spice I wasn't used to causing a bit of a stir but in my DOOMSDAY brain I had a sudden fear that I was going to get full-blown food poisoning right-here, right then.

Physically I felt OK but because I was thinking about how awful it would be to feel sick I started to actually *feel* sick. My stomach seemed to curdle and I could feel something wanting to creep up my throat. I tried to focus on what my date was saying instead of my intense nausea, but he was giving me a really detailed description of his new road bike and it was far too boring to keep my attention. I spotted a bin a few feet behind him and excused myself to go throw away my empty curry box. He offered to take mine but I insisted, possibly too firmly, that I'd do it.

At the bin I threw our boxes in really deep so I could lean over. I used this as an excuse to potentially vomit out whatever my body was dismissing. I told my body if it really wanted to puke it could do it now relatively unnoticed. I opened my mouth, hunched over even further but apart from a dry-heave that I masked as a cough nothing came out. I stumbled over to my date and suggested we go for a walk. I spotted a corner shop and went in for a bottle of water.

When I finally held the bottle to my lips the cool liquid

felt like it was extinguishing a fire in a burning building. The sickly curry taste subsided, my nausea faded, I felt calm. I offered him some and he took a big swig: 'Oh I needed that!' I laughed. The irony.

From this point on I always carry water with me wherever I go. Whether it's a date, a job interview, a train journey, a bike ride. Water is so unequivocally good for you, you know the second it hits your body you're doing a good thing.

Dating also involves not dating. The bits in between where you're worrying, stressing out, figuring out how and when to respond. If things have gone well and a second date is on the cards I hover around my phone like a thirsty animal hangs around a spring. It's a life source. If I get a text from my date I'll feel instantly better, energised and happy about the world. If the well's run dry and he's a no-show I feel miserable and rejected.

After being ghosted millions of times I've succumbed to the school of 'He's Just Not That Into You' – a phrase made famous by the self-help book from the early 2000s of the same title and a subsequent film that's not great. I read the book for the first time when I was fifteen. A fellow emo music enthusiast I met on MySpace didn't respond to my messages and I brushed it off with an 'Oh Well, He's Not That Into You'. I've repeated that phrase over and over throughout my dating life. It has been helpful in that it has allowed me to shrug off deadbeat guys instantly, but it has been unhelpful in that I have said it too often and too quickly. Even if a guy took an hour instead of ten minutes to reply to a text I'd say that out loud like a mantra. I'd be breaking up with the guy before we even started dating.

When my now boyfriend Alex and I were arranging one of our earlier dates, there was a point at which it had been a week and a bit since we'd last seen each other. I was in the height of my 'Yep, pretty sure this guy doesn't like me' phase. He'd not read some of my WhatsApp messages whilst he *had* been online so I'd assumed he was off boning the rest of London and had forgotten to keep me informed. He was too hot for me anyway. It just wasn't going to happen.

To my surprise he got in touch on a Friday night after he'd come back from a work trip to ask how my night was going. At that time I was in the back of an Uber going home from the pub. Alex and I sent a few back and forth texts about our respective evenings and somewhere in the middle of the conversation we apparently arranged to meet up the next day. I went to bed feeling happy and excited.

When I woke up it was as if my memory had been wiped. Our conversation had been swallowed up in the black hole of my 'everything is awful' thinking. Because I'd spent a few weeks stewing in this feeling of 'Oh he definitely doesn't like me', I'd gotten too used to it, like a hoodie that smells and makes you look a bit square-shaped but you wear it anyway because you've had it for ages and it's sort of comfortable.

A friend of mine called me in the morning and asked what I was doing with my day and I moaned about how this guy I really liked wasn't really reciprocating and I thought we'd have another date by now but it's just not going to happen, woe is me, etc., etc., etc. She told me to go back to bed. Wait a few hours. Text him and if he didn't get back I'd go to her house and we'd do something fun.

We hung up. I put *Seinfeld* on and grabbed a bag of Doritos. This was going to be my Saturday now. At 1pm I got a text from Alex: 'Hey, running five minutes late. See you soon!'

Soon?

Sooon?

SOOOOOON????

My heart crashed into the pit of my stomach. Where was he going? What did he mean he was running late? Where were we meeting? Why didn't I realise we'd made a plan? I raced through our text message exchange and it hit me. 1pm. Somerset House. It was right there. Flashing at me. Fuck Fuck Fuck Fuck Fuck.

At the time my flat was 90 minutes away from Somerset House by train and I'd used my monthly. 'Fuck it just get an Uber' allowance on the night before. I texted a thousand apologies to Alex hoping desperately he wouldn't be offended by my lateness. Because he's an actual nice normal person he said not to worry. He was going to do some shopping and he'd wait for me in the cafe.

That was one problem sorted but I looked in the mirror and realised I had another dilemma. Doritos dust speckled my cheek. My hair was a matt from yesterday's dry shampoo and London Underground dirt. I wiped my face with my T-shirt. I took a make-up brush and some powder and covered up most of the grease on my face. A quick change into a dress, some deodorant and chewing gum and I ran out of the door.

Imagine if my brain wasn't wired to automatically assume the worst in a situation. Instead of rushing I could have had a wonderful, relaxing Saturday morning, with plenty of time to get ready and feel confident. Instead, I had to sprint through London with sweat cascading out of my armpits.

YOU DON'T HAVE TO TELL ANYONE ABOUT YOUR MENTAL HEALTH

If your mental health condition impacts your day-to-day life you might feel inclined to share what you're going through with whomever you're dating. When, where and how you do this is entirely up to you. It's your information. You own it. No one can force you to give anything away you don't want to.

When I was at a friend's pub lock-in for her thirty-eighth birthday I was stuck talking to an Irish pastry chef. I say stuck because the pub is shaped liked a narrow corridor. Once you're standing next to someone that's kind of your spot for the rest of the night. So from the get-go not a great location for someone with anxiety.

Pastry Chef was bald, with deep-sea blue eyes and a tribal tattoo around his bicep. He asked me what I did for a living. I told him that I write.

'What kind of stuff do you write?'

'Mainly pieces on mental health.'

'Oh. OH.'

He took a step back like I'd just spat out a dirty word and a warning sign flared between us. This was not going to be a guy I was going to get along with. He then went on to make it even worse: 'Oh I know some real mental girls. Like REALLY mental.'

Firstly, this man was in his forties, AKA a grown-ass man. You should know better to not refer to women as 'girls' unless you are literally talking about a child, which he wasn't. Then there's the fact that in his statement he drew that dividing line between him (a sane person) and all these women he supposedly knows (the crazies), implying that they were in the wrong and he was a victim.

Pastry Chef detected a slight eye-roll in my expression and began to excuse his statement by telling me all about his ex who had bipolar and how she's ruined his life. 'She should have told me she was bipolar. I should have been prepared.' I didn't know what to say to that. I had only just met him. I felt like I didn't want him to unload his and his ex's history on me. He decided to change gear: 'Do you write from experience then?' I nodded. 'What's wrong with you?' He said this in a jokey way making his blue eyes glow but I was not going to fall for it that easily. 'Nothing's wrong with me. I have borderline personality disorder with a side of depression and anxiety.' I then did an over-the-top curtsey and looked around me for an escape route, but he still wasn't quite done.

'Do you tell people you date you have mental problems?'

'Eventually I guess.'

'But the first date?'

'I don't know.'

'You should tell them.'

'Why?'

'Else it's false advertising.'

'Huh?'

'If they don't know what's wrong with you then it's like you're lying.'

At this point the anger that had been slowly festering in my belly spread all throughout my body. I wanted to scream in this man's face, show him my full-blown crazy lady but instead I swallowed my anger and escaped to the bathroom where I published a series of angry tweets about the situation. I knew he wouldn't listen to me, or maybe I was too exhausted to try and a crowded corridor-shaped pub just wasn't the place to do it. I avoided him for the rest of the night and when I got home punched my pillow a few times.

Not telling the person I'm on a first date with that I have mental health issues is not 'false advertising'. There's more to people than whatever is going on inside of their heads. Yes, sometimes that part of my life does take over and things go wobbly. Sometimes things might get so bad that relationships end or I end up hurting people, but for the most part I'm just me. I'm on a date wanting to tell you about my life, the good parts, the interesting parts and the parts I think are more important.

When I fill someone in on my mental health issues it's always in a place where I'm beginning to fully trust them. I know that there's longevity in our relationship, it's not just a series of drunken stumblings out of pubs.

I've been incredibly fortunate that no one has reacted badly to me sharing my issues. If I can tell that the person is going to be shifty or weird about it I probably wouldn't be attracted to them in the first place. I had a drink with someone who was talking about their ex and referring to her multiple times as a 'psycho' and I thought nope, this one isn't for me. That's not the kind of guy I want to date. Maybe she wasn't great, maybe she did do some inappropriate things but I don't know the full story. I'd hate the idea of being confined to one person's unkind description of me.

7

REMEMBER THIS WHEN YOU'RE HAVING SEX

Sex is great. Orgasms are great. When someone kisses you so passionately you lose yourself and stars begin to waltz around your head and everything is dreamy and lovely, that too is great. However, it's not always like this.

I've launched myself into sex so quickly, there's not a lot of passion involved. It's hard, fast, painful and destructive. I've used my body like a sex doll, hoping someone can bring it to life again. Sex won't bring it to life – self-care and self-respect and genuinely being OK will bring it to life. Having someone thrust their fingers inside me so deep it hurts isn't me enjoying myself or having a great time. I'm self-harming, and I'm using someone else to do it.

Having borderline personality disorder makes casual sex difficult too. I feel things very intensely very quickly and the guy who I met at a house party who I fuck but have zero things in common with can quickly become the absolute best man in the world and OMG I cannot wait for our children to pop out of my vagina. Even without borderline personality disorder I'm a hopeless romantic. I like the idea of meet-cutes and love at first sight. I want an instant connection but I want it so much that I force it at times.

In my worst moments I've resorted to sex in the futile hope to 'feel' something again. I'd fuck people I knew were bad for me, but in my head I dressed them up as saviours. I'd give my entire body to them and define myself in their gaze. I'd be a sucker for bullshit compliments and pick-up lines. I've met up with guys who had girlfriends and I didn't care. I've met guys who'd say things like, 'I don't normally do this' and not cared that this was probably a fabricated line they told everyone. I got them to come home with me, and told myself that surely this means there's something good about me.

I became hooked on having sex with people in this meaningless, vapid way, all the while hoping secretly it would lead to something more. I'd sleep with an ex and 'fuckboys' I didn't know and flirt with sleazy divorced men. In my mind it was possible something could happen out of these encounters, but once the spell was over I'd go home cursing myself for being the way I am. That married man I made out with on the District Line is definitely not going to be the one to save me from myself. Especially not with his hand up my skirt or his tongue down my throat.

This period of my life felt a lot like I was running around London, glass of wine in hand trying to find myself. I look at the clothes I bought in this time, all tight, black dresses; booby and high-heeled. There's nothing wrong with donning your tightest dress and hitting the town when you feel like it, but I was doing this every night. I was defining myself by how much I could get people to want to have sex with me. I wanted so much to feel safe and secure but instead sabotaged my safety by making bad decisions.

I still haven't quite figured out how to differentiate good sex and bad sex. You're not always going to have sex with someone you love so that can't be the defining trademark. I feel like a lot of it has to do with trusting your gut. The feeling deep down in your belly that knows what's wrong and what's right – or at the very least what feels safe. I've ditched perfectly lovely evenings with friends because some guy I didn't care about texted me a picture of his dick and wanted me to meet up with him. In my head I felt like that would be more beneficial for me, that I'd get something out of it. In hindsight having a quiet night with friends, talking and, making jokes, would have been so much better.

I'm learning how to make better decisions for myself, and how to protect myself in doing so. I'm trying to give a voice to that feeling that says, 'This isn't OK' and act on it when I hear it. I'm lucky in that I have a boyfriend now who I have a brilliant and very sexual relationship with. If I say 'no' it's an immediate no, there's no pressure, and at no point do I feel obliged to do something I don't have to do. I feel like this might be very 'Yeah, duh! That should be the norm!' to a lot of people. And it should, but when your sense of self has been obliterated by depression and self-destruction it's not always easy to demand the things you know are right for you. It's a learning process, and one I feel like I'm finally getting the hang of.

REMEMBER THiS
WhEN YOU'RE iN A
RELaTIONShIP

Well done! You've survived the mindfuck that's dating and you're in a proper hold-hands-when-you're-walking-down-the-street kind of relationship. Unless you're like me and holding hands makes you recoil. Then maybe you link pinkies or touch each other's fingertips every now and again. Either way, you're in it. You've found someone you love spending time with. You hang out often. You have sex. Your friends think they're great and then the inevitable happens. That great period in the beginning of every relationship, where everything is fun and easy becomes less bright. Like an old T-shirt that loses its colour in the wash, things feel a little less sparkly between the two of you (bear with it though because old T-shirts are always my fave and get worn the most).

You might start bickering more, you cry in front of each other for the first time and some of your behaviours that you hated about yourself in past relationships crawl back in: whether it's paranoia, insecurity, jealousy, being a nit-picker, etc.

Part of it is inevitable because if two people spend a lot of time together they get to know each other. Not the surface-level stuff but the stuff underneath it all – the stuff that troubles you and that scares you – and it can't all be pretty.

It's this part of a relationship I find super hard to navigate because I'm such an ALL OR NOTHING person. If I'm arguing with someone, even if it's just a little quibble, in my head we are shouting at each other and we might as well just break up because this is so awful see you later bye! I'm so quick to write things off and it's not because I want to, it's because deep down there's a distinct feeling that I don't deserve to be loved. It sounds super dramatic and emo but if there's a thing about me that someone wanting to be my partner should know it's that. It's where all my weird behaviours stem from. I genuinely feel that there's something so inherently off about me that anyone who says they love me must be full of absolute shit, or worse: I've tricked them.

I try my very best to fight against this feeling and the more I'm honest about it to the person I'm with the better. I might freak out about something really mundane and it's not because I'm overly insecure or jealous – I don't actually think they're about to run off with that hot girl they keep liking on Instagram. It's because my brain is gathering evidence to support my hypothesis: no one can love me. Some relationships make it easier to gather this kind of evidence. I have been with people who have cheated on me, or not cheated but pretty much cheated. On the flipside I've been in relationships that have actually been good and yet I spin them around to fit my theory that they don't love me.

It's how I've blitzed through a series of relationships over the past couple of years. Repeating the pattern of dating someone, falling in love, having them say they love me and then working my way to make them fall out of love because I never really believed them in the first place.

Love to me seems like a bar of soap that keeps slipping out of my hands. Each time I think I know what it is its definition changes completely. Every time I think I'm in love I feel like this is nothing like it was before, this time it's love, like love-love, and that thing a year ago must have been something else.

When a relationship with a painter called M. ended in an emotional disaster I decided I needed to do something about the way I was bulldozing my way through relationships. M. was someone I probably shouldn't have gotten with. We were housemates and it was all very awkward and close. We called it a day after I told him I didn't think he was really into me and we were fighting too much. He didn't agree with the first part but agreed with the latter. It ended quite amicably until I jumped back into dating the following day, which wasn't really ideal. Because of our close proximity he realised what I'd been up to and wrote me an email that was pretty much '10 Things I Hate About You' but actual things he hated, not things he thought were secretly cute.

He said he hated me for being a toxic bitch, for manipulating his feelings and for being selfish. It was like seeing everything I hated about myself splashed on a billboard in Piccadilly Circus. I was confronted with the ugly truth of my personality, or at least how my personality navigated this relationship. In convincing myself he didn't really care about me I'd prevented us from having a genuine relationship.

Even as we broke up I thought: 'Ah, he won't care about this, this is nothing to him.' Never did I think actually this might affect him, this might make him feel sad. I never considered him to have any feelings about me. I realised I wasn't the victim of all my failed relationships; I had orchestrated their breakdown (well, most of them). I had pushed people away and ignored their side of things.

Changing my relationship ways hasn't been the easiest

thing in the world. I do sometimes run down the street crying over a problem I've created in my head but I'm also learning that that isn't solely my fault. Feeling deeply unlovable is lonely, and it's shitty and it's tiring. I didn't wake up and choose to feel like that. I don't carry that feeling around with me on purpose because it's fun or interesting. It's carrying a bunch of dead weight for no reason. It's in my way, it gets in other people's way. I hate it.

Thanks to therapy and having a boyfriend I really, really want to make all the effort in the world for, I'm learning to forgive myself for past relationship fuck-ups. I'm learning to stop thinking of myself as the worst/ugliest/smelliest/dumbest person ever. I'm learning that I have something good to add to a relationship. I'm a good partner. I care about people. I can make people happy. It's not a big magic trick; it's real and it's possible.

I've also tried to devise a little checklist for when my brain is ready to jump to conclusions. (Caveat: sometimes jumping to conclusions is the right thing to do, like when I spotted a guy I was dating religiously liking everything a female colleague of ours was doing on Instagram and BAM! after he dumped me they ended up together. However, generally, that isn't how it works.) When I can feel a little spark in the pit of my stomach making me feel like unwanted drama is on the

119

horizon, I try my hardest to pause for just one little second and go through this handy list:

- Stop what you're thinking about before the spiral of thoughts continues. Just stop for a second and examine those thoughts – what's going on? What's worrying you? What are you afraid of?

- Voice some of the thoughts out loud. I'm luckily dating someone now who is the most patient man in the world so he's OK with me asking him a million questions a day. This is how a typical convo will go:

  Me: Do you love me?

  Him: Yes.

  Me: But do you like me?

  Him: Yeah, of course.

  Me: But do you like me as an actual person?

  Him: Yes.

  Me: OK. Pizza?

- Don't lump all the people you've ever dated in one big ball. Sometimes patterns develop in a relationship that you might recognise from a relationship before, and if they're valid warning signs – like they make you feel bad about yourself – then you need to absolutely listen to those, but if they're just little everyday things don't think: 'Oh, my ex used to tell me off for leaving

my clothes all over the floor, here we go again,
another guy trying to change me, oh my god
all men are terrible.' Now I just say: 'Look, I'm a
messy person, I'll tidy when I feel like it, there's
no point trying to get me to change.' That way
the progression of the relationship can go in
its own direction rather than just following the
course of my past ones where tiny fights about
me being messy escalate tenfold

9

REMEMBER THIS
WhEN SOMEONE ELSE
HUrTS YOU

Relationships, the good ones at least, are about letting people disarm your steely wall of self-protection because you feel comfortable and safe. You're getting to know each other and you feel comfortable showing them other parts of your life they haven't seen before.

To get to this point you need a good understanding of what your own boundaries are because you can't always choose who enters your life and in what shape they'll exit it. People who are good to you will listen to your cues and leave when you want them to, but they'll stay put when you need help. In short: they respect your boundaries.

As a very simplified definition, boundaries tend to be physical or psychological. Your physical boundary is pretty self-explanatory – the barrier between you and someone or something else. Psychological boundaries are complex. In the essay 'The Unthinkable Boundaries of Self' Professor Ciarán Benson writes that psychological boundaries are tied up with acts of possessing or of owning. They include what belongs to you (things, people, ideas, skills, rights, reputations, privileges, etc.). Essentially: things you control and call your own. They also encompass the way in which you belong to others (forms of solidarity, group identity, obligation, etc.) that control and have claim on you. In this sense, what people own, and how they are themselves owned, helps make them the sort of people they are.

When you're sensitive or anxious or you've experienced trauma in your life, you might have a complicated relationship with your psychological boundaries. There's a push – pull in terms of what you feel you have ownership over, and how others have ownership over you.

I have steely walls I set up to protect myself from the outside world. It's such a mess in my head that my boundaries are largely there for self-preservation. I need room to reinstate some kind of equilibrium. If people come too close they could throw me off my game even more. However, sometimes I push too hard and I'm left in a lonely room in my brain with an aching longing for companionship, but it's too late to let someone in.

When someone oversteps my boundaries by doing something I'm not comfortable with I retreat even further into myself. I shut down. The space I choose to take up in this world becomes smaller, I become smaller; my hopes and demands and my voice all shrink at once.

It's in these moments I try to recall someone who to me had the right idea. Someone who defended her boundaries like a proud landowner shooing away poachers.

I was accompanying Antonia, a Greek classmate, on a shopping trip to the mall. She was my age, fourteen at the time. Her hair was dusty blonde, she had a belly button ring and wore neon laces in her Converse. She had a spark, and whenever I saw her she seemed to possess a confidence most teenage girls lacked. Her dusty blonde hair was always ironed straight and she flicked it often like she was flinging a handbag over her shoulder. Despite being considerably taller than her, my long lanky legs struggled to keep up with her quick stride.

We were walking through the food court to reach the escalators at the end of the mall. She wanted to get some new hoop earrings. I wanted to get whatever she was getting. Anything that could get me closer to being a little bit more like her.

A large group of older boys passed us and I clenched my fist knowing what was about to come. At the very least they'd make some kind of remark; at the worst they'd try to touch us. This shopping mall had become a hotspot for sexual harassment. Boys at least five years older than me would touch my arm, my butt or follow me around as I tried to find the exit. I still went back though. My lust for Dunkin' Donuts surpassed the stress of having my body poked and prodded. I had learnt to always wear long skirts in the mall, brush my long fringe over my face and tie my jumper around my waist to hide any curves.

Despite my armour of layers I knew we'd be no match for this large group of pulsating testosterone. The guys passed us and to no one's surprise sucked their tongues and said something I couldn't hear but it was bound to be rude. I closed my eyes and increased my pace hoping Antonia would do the same. Antonia did the opposite. The boys slowed down and she stopped right in front of them. She stared the leader of the pack straight in the eyes: 'NO!' she shouted at him. Her voice wasn't shrill or scared, it was firm and strong and delightfully terrifying. 'DON'T DO THAT AGAIN.' She took my hand and we marched further along the mall, down the escalators and straight to Claire's Accessories. I wanted to hug her but she was too busy looking for earrings. Antonia hadn't done anything out of the ordinary for her. She'd recognised an uncomfortable situation and stood up for herself. She used her voice to reaffirm her boundary. She told anyone who wanted to fuck with her that they couldn't overstep the line. She wouldn't let them.

I wanted with every fibre of my being to soak up some of Antonia's badassery but never quite got there. My 'NO' was never loud like Antonia's, but more a meek whisper. I didn't know how to sound like her.

A week later I was in that same shopping mall with my mum. We took the escalator together, she was in front and behind me a man lifted up my school skirt and put his entire hand on my bum before walking up the escalator out of sight. My body had frozen in place. I wanted to scream. The spot where he'd left his hand felt like it was burning through me. I hated him. I wanted to find him and punch him. I was so angry I wanted to run through the mall with a baseball bat and smash things to pieces.

But I couldn't do anything. I felt ashamed. I felt ashamed of my own silence, which only grew worse. My mum asked if I wanted something to eat and I asked if we could go home instead. I knew Antonia wouldn't have let this happen. If only she had been there.

I never found out how to unleash my inner Antonia — in fact my boundaries have become more inflexible as I have grown older. They are watertight. I don't like being touched. I don't like it when people sit too close to me. There's a forcefield around me.

Through doing that arduous task of growing up, I

realised how boundaries can be tied up to your emotional space that often manifests itself in what you choose to reveal to people. When I'm nervous I have no problem making fun of myself, often sharing an inappropriate story to do with sex or farting or falling over. It's a way to laugh at myself before anyone else can.

So on the outside it seems like I'm pretty chilled about everything, but really I'm over sharing to the point where I'm turning myself into a joke. I don't want anyone to take me too seriously. This is a very 2-D version of me. And by projecting that person I'm shutting people out. I'm putting out a funnier version of myself and drawing the vulnerable person back in. 'You won't believe this really fucking stupid thing I did last week!' is my own personal smokescreen. I'm telling people to go look at that other person waving their arms about frantically. Don't look at the woman in the corner. Leave that woman alone.

If all this talk about boundaries has you confused here's a list of some of the times I felt people disrespected my boundaries in small, sometimes even barely noticeable, ways so you can see what I mean:

- When someone (usually a man) yells, 'Oi darling, give us a smile!' I don't have a choice whether or not I want to hear his order because he's literally right in my ear

- When I'm sitting with someone who finds it funny that I hate being physically close to people so they move their chair right in front of my face
- When I was fourteen and some boys at school cornered me in the locker room asking if I'd ever fingered myself
- When someone I didn't know very well sent me a photo of their penis without me asking
- When I'm meeting up with an old boyfriend and we're having a nice catch-up but out of the blue he leans in for a kiss and I almost tumble off my chair to avoid having his mouth land on my face
- When a man on the Tube decides to stand even closer to me so he can look down my top
- When someone repeatedly asks me questions about my sex life when the conversation isn't about sex at all
- When someone tells me a massive secret that I didn't ask for
- When I'm in a group and someone decides to tell my story to the group as if it's theirs
- When I'm tickled
- When I get pulled onto someone's lap
- When someone shakes my hand and puts their other hand onto our handshake making it like a hand prison

- When someone shows up at my house after I've told them I want space
- When someone acts like they're my therapist and tries to diagnose me
- When someone assumes something about me without checking first
- When someone reads my diaries
- When someone goes through my inbox
- When someone gives me unsolicited advice
- When someone tells me they think I should come off my meds

THE REALLY, REALLY BAD THING THAT HAPPENED

What I'm about to tell you was the most difficult part of this book. I wrote it all down because it was a reminder to myself that despite the cage of boundaries I set up, self-protection can be limited. Sometimes people break through, they force their way in and they hurt you more than you ever thought was possible.

Nearly half a million adults are sexually assaulted in England and Wales each year. After it happened to me I felt unsafe, I felt ashamed and I felt like it was my fault. Slowly I patched myself up, not completely because the thread still unravels sometimes, but I did eventually learn to trust people again.

The night of my assault was doomed from the start.

I was twenty-six. Post break-up, post trying to set my arm on fire outside the pub, I had plasters on my skin but my life still had many cracks in it. I needed change desperately and whilst I was being proactive I'd had one of those days that seemed to be an assembly line of bad news.

I'd had two job interviews, and both seemed extremely promising. However, both interviewers called me one after the other that day to tell me I hadn't made the cut; they liked me but someone else was better suited. I slumped into my therapist's chair at 5pm completely deflated. She had some news of her own: she was pregnant. The pregnancy was likely going to be quite rough due to several complications and she needed to stop working. I leapt up and congratulated her but she gently nudged me to sit back down again.

'Do you understand what this means for our sessions?'

I did a slow nod which she rightly interpreted as a no. I didn't realise this would be the end of the road for us. I'd have to choose a new therapist and I'd have to start again with someone else. Deep down I also felt a sense of rejection, like she was choosing her baby over me. I should have used this opportunity to voice these concerns but instead I just shrugged and said I was so happy for her.

I ignored the thunderbolt of panic that struck my chest. I ignored the worry; the fear that I'd have nowhere else to go. I'd come to depend on these weekly sessions. I'd store up all the worries whizzing around my head and pour them out slowly drop-by-drop whenever we met. I liked her a lot. She was kind and warm and foreign in London like me, but she was leaving me. In a few weeks I'd never see her again.

Once I was out of my session I smoked a few cigarettes and walked to the National Portrait Gallery where I was meeting an old friend I hadn't seen in years. We'd spotted we both lived in London on Facebook and decided to meet up for a drink. At this point I was caught up in a lot of dating drama and thought it would be a relief to spend an evening with an old friend. It would be safe and pleasant and fun, like meeting up with a cousin.

On my way to the museum I recognised the man in front of me and almost tripped over my own feet. It was my ex-boyfriend. I darted into an alleyway and peered round the wall to spy on him. It had to be him: same hair, same shoes, same stockish way of standing. I didn't want to say hi, especially not if he saw I was meeting a guy friend. I didn't want him to think I'd moved on. I didn't want to give him another reason to hate me.

I crouched down a bit lower and kept staring. He was checking his phone and walking towards me. 'Fuck,' I thought. I turned away and stood up straight. If he was going to bump into me I at least needed to make it seem like I hadn't been stalking him. My heart was pounding. I felt nervous and sick. I wanted to light another cigarette but my hands were too shaky. 'Just stand here,' I thought. 'Just stand here and be cool.' I plucked up the courage to turn around ready to say hi. When he was about an arm's length away from me it struck me that this man wasn't my ex at all. He was just some guy. Relief flooded my body, but I felt extremely stupid. All that adrenaline for nothing.

My friend arrived and we hugged and I told him my lame story about not bumping into my ex. He guided us to a pub. I was so desperate for a drink it was like I'd been out in the desert and I'd finally spotted a water tank. I hadn't realised my friend had booked a fancy restaurant in Soho for after the pub. I thought this night would just be a couple of drinks and then that's it. I ordered another large glass of wine and thought, 'Fuck it.' I'd had a shit day, I knew he was kind of loaded and would probably pay for the dinner and I wanted to make the most of this.

At the restaurant I drank more. I wasn't engaged in our conversation. I was thinking about my job situation, my ex and all the wine I was still planning on drinking. There were times in my conversation with my friend that felt a bit off. He touched my wrist at one point. Gently nudged my knee with his hand. Stared at my face for a second too long that made me think, 'Wait, this isn't just friendly any more.' I was getting drunker and my feelings of discomfort were pushed aside by intoxication.

After dinner I wanted to go home but he suggested we go for one more drink. In the pub I drank more and then in another pub I drank more still. From this point on my memory stops. Thinking back to it is like staring into a bucket of black paint. There's nothing there. I can't see a thing.

When I regained consciousness I could feel that I was in a bed. I was horizontal. There were sheets beneath me. The ceiling was white, the window was open and it was morning. There was a sharp pain in my lower body. I opened my eyes. My friend's naked body was thrusting in and out of me. My insides were completely dry. It felt less like sex and more like scraping. I closed my eyes again. Last night's alcohol twinged my stomach. This wasn't happening. I couldn't have this happen to me. I needed to say no, I needed to make a sound but I couldn't. I couldn't open my mouth. I squeezed my eyes shut and escaped back into my head. I thought if I could just drift outside of my body maybe my body could disappear too.

When I found myself fully disconnected from the lifeless blob of flesh being fucked below me I found I wasn't the only person hovering over my body, I had company. There was my ex I thought I'd seen the day before and his mum and his dad and his sister and her husband. There were all the people I knew I'd hurt when I broke up with my ex. I imagined them standing there cheering the act on, wanting it to hurt, telling me I deserved this. They were a Greek chorus of hate. I knew none of these people would ever want this to happen to me but in my hallucination it felt extremely real. It felt what was happening to my body below was justified.

When the man I thought was my friend finally stopped he laid down and trapped me in a sweaty hug. I re-entered my body. I felt the bristle of hair on his chest. I could smell his sweat, his morning breath. I hated it. I hated everything but I still felt unable to move. My mind and body hadn't fully connected yet.

I slid out of his embrace and went to his bathroom where I dry-heaved into the toilet. I couldn't throw up. I wanted to purge the terrible evening but I wasn't able to. He asked if I was OK and I said I was going to go home. I tried to pee but everything ached down there. It felt like someone had shoved sandpaper inside me. I put my clothes on and switched the autopilot part of my brain on. I had to get home. I had to get through this.

I remember being walked to the bus stop. I remember trying hard to be friendly. I remember he hugged me goodbye and I could feel the vomit rise again. I remember getting on the bus only to get off again. I remember a McDonald's loo. I remember staring at some gum stuck on a wall. I remember getting back on the bus. I remember getting home, taking my clothes off and wrapping myself up in a duvet.

I remember feeling like something awful had happened but I wasn't quite sure what.

WHAT TO DO AFTER

After that night it felt like someone had knocked all the insides out of my body. If you tapped my skull you could hear the echo reverberate to my toes: I was empty. The parts of my brain controlling everyday things like appetite and tiredness had tangled together into a knot. I didn't know what was going on, what I was doing or what I was feeling.

I told the story of that night to myself over and over and even branched out to a few close friends. I hoped that by imposing a narrative on that blurred evening I could turn it into something that made sense, something I could manage, but every time I divulged a bit of information or made the story more real it became harder for me to believe. Did this really happen? Am I *sure* it's not my fault? I was the one drinking. Did I do this?

I wish there had been some kind of guide, or a quiz, to help marshal the flurry of worries that consumed me. Did you black out? Yes. Go straight to question 3. Did it hurt? Yes. Go to your GP now. Was it unprotected? Yes. Go to the sexual health clinic.

It took me a while and a lot of stumbling through a flurry of mixed-up thought processes to finally come to terms with the fact that I didn't give consent. It was sexual assault. I was unconscious. I've spoken to men who have been with me when I've passed out and they told me it's like rolling a blob of jelly down the street. I'm completely gone. I might mutter the odd word but it's clear I'm incoherent and not really there. That man had sex with me against my will.

Everyone's experience of sexual violence is different, so unfortunately there can't be a blueprint for what to do after it's happened, but here are some things I have learnt that might be helpful if you've been through this too:

1. WHATEVER YOU'RE DOING, IT'S OK

There is no one-size-fits-all reaction. Whether you find yourself climbing the walls, shouting in your pillow, swearing at people who are trying to support you – these are acceptable reactions. A lot of my responses trickled in a lot later and I found myself lashing out at people who were helping me. I was dating someone who was patient with me and yet after we'd have sex I'd cry and call him terrible names, as if all my anger was directed at him not the attacker.

I felt extremely guilty for my behaviour during this time but after speaking to psychologist Dr Nina Burrowes I realised that whatever I had to do, I simply had to do it. You have to give yourself permission to go through the inevitable emotional rollercoaster. The more you stifle yourself, the bumpier that rollercoaster can get. Dr Burrowes also shared with me an incredible piece of advice that kept coming back to me: have compassion for yourself. Whatever you're doing, it's your way of dealing with it. You've got to give yourself some slack.

2. DON'T FORCE YOURSELF TO DO ANYTHING YOU DON'T WANT TO DO

I was reluctant to confront the guy who did this to me, but I did feel some kind of responsibility to make sure he would never hurt anyone ever again. Perhaps this would give me some closure too? There's a lot of talk, especially on American TV, about victims forgiving their attacker. Thing is, I had no desire to forgive him or to school him on his actions. My main desire was to avoid this person for the rest of my life. I didn't want to have to see him. I didn't want to talk with him.

I imagined myself walking into a cafe if I did arrange a meet up. I imagined how nervous I'd feel. How nauseous. How sweaty my palms would get. Just picturing my body in the same room as his body made my stomach twist. Breathing the same air. What if I could smell him? What if I dissociated on the spot? What if I retreated so far into my mind I'd never come back? What if I got drunk? What if I lost control? What if it happened again?

I lectured myself on what I believed to be my duty: my duty to confront this man was more important than my own well-being. I scolded myself for being weak and lazy. But despite my own negative self-talk I still couldn't motivate myself to type his number into my phone. After a year of this wrestling match between what I felt I had to do and what I wanted to do I finally deleted his number. Perhaps in a few years I'll be ready, and I'll get that number back, but right now I want to let myself live. I'm not lazy, I'm proactively putting my own mental health first. I'm letting go of invisible pressures. I'm taking it one day at a time, on my own terms.

3. TELL PEOPLE WHEN YOU'RE READY

It's not easy starting that process of saying out loud what happened to you. You don't just have your own feelings to consider, you're thinking about the other person too: will they believe me? How will they take this? Will they be OK?

If you want to talk to someone about what you've been through, make sure it's the right person. Just as it's vital to have compassion for yourself during this time, you have to have the headspace to have compassion for the person you're sharing your story with. It's shocking and upsetting to hear that someone you care about has been violated. If you're able to, give them space to be able to react. Try not to set them up to fail. Don't go in there with too many expectations. If you have specific needs from someone tell them that from the outset, for example: 'I would really like you to come to the police station with me' or 'I just really need someone to sit with me for a bit.' That way they have a framework to work with and they'll know how to support you.

I think my biggest mistake was rushing into telling people what had happened without knowing what I wanted from them. Perhaps it would have helped if I'd said: 'Look I'm telling you this, I don't really know why, I don't know how I need you to react so just give me some time.' Instead, I blurted my story out and declared the conversation was closed, I didn't want to talk any more. I then grew angry and resentful when that person hadn't acted in the way I wanted them to, which was unfair.

If you're the person hearing this story for the first time, I'd say the most important thing is to not say anything at all – just listen. Make sure you're making your friend or relative feel safe.

4. THERE'S NO DEADLINE

With physical trauma you might be told that you need rest and you'll be able to walk on your sprained ankle in a week or two. Emotional healing is a slower journey. It might feel long and drawn-out in parts and other times it might feel stifling and panicky. The most important thing is to give yourself permission to breathe and to find your own pace. I'm still dealing with what happened to me, I still think about it. Scenes flash into my head when I see a blonde-haired man in a suit. I once dry-heaved into my backpack when my night bus drove past the place where it all happened.

Just when you think you've got the hang of your trauma, there's a strong possibility that your pace will change. Sometimes you'll feel like you're sprinting towards recovery. I joined a group training session on how to watch out for signs of domestic abuse in your community. To me this felt like retaliation. I felt triumphant. I was going to help someone, or at least try. But other times I feel completely consumed by fear and shame, like I've taken a million steps back.

Often this happens arbitrarily. I was watching a TV show where a character played by Nicole Kidman gets repeatedly abused, but the situation is murky in the beginning, and there's an insinuation that part of her welcomes the abuse. During one of the episodes it felt like a spotlight had been turned on above me. I felt like I could relate to her character, even though it was such an extreme version of what I'd been through. If people at any point think Kidman's character was to blame, what about me? Surely they'd think the same. In that moment I went from eating Doritos in my bed to spinning out of control and resorting to my crutch: leaving the house and trading my Doritos in for two bottles of cornershop wine.

Dr Burrowes told me that life after abuse is a bit like grief. It's something you learn to live with and that process isn't easy. A lot of it has to do with striking a balance and slowly figuring out what you're comfortable with. What happened to you deserves all the compassion in the world, it's not an easy thing to get over. It's fucked up and it's catastrophically unfair but many people can expect to fully recover from trauma.

On a good day it does help for me to put things into the context of my whole life. The assault isn't going to redefine everything I've been through so far and it's not going to define what's yet to come.

5. YOU AREN'T OBLIGATED TO DO ANYTHING

After a rape, you might feel it's important to report what's happened to you. There can be several motivations for this. The fact remains that reporting assault isn't easy, there's a tremendous amount of labour involved, which you're expected to carry out on top of the pressure of having to deal with trauma.

The criminal justice system expects the world from you. Make sure reporting your incident is absolutely what you want. If you want the person to face charges and you know that that process itself will be empowering to you, then it's a good move.

If possible, gather a good support network around you that have your back. You might need people to lift you up in times where it all gets overwhelming.

There are people who have reported their assault

and had good experiences: they were listened to and ultimately they were vindicated. However, not everyone has the outcome they hoped for. The process is draining and will differ depending on what country you're in. In the UK the National Rape Crisis helpline is a good starting point and in the US you'll want to check out RAINN (Rape, Abuse & Incest National Network). If the assault happened recently, go to the police station as soon as possible and take someone you trust. You might be examined for evidence which can include saliva, blood and urine samples. Photographs might be taken and it's very likely you'll be encouraged to have a test for any sexual transmitted diseases.

In the UK the Crown Persecution Service are the ones who decide if there's enough evidence for a prosecution to go to court. If there's a lack of evidence they'll say no. It doesn't mean they don't believe you, it means legally they can't see enough evidence for a conviction. It's little consolation but it's vital that you remember you did everything possible.

6. GUILT IS A COPING MECHANISM

I spent a lot of time flip-flopping between rage against the perpetrator and rage against myself. I told myself I probably led him on. I reminded myself of how drunk I can get and I even concluded that even if it was rape I probably deserved it anyway.

The guilt was relentless and exhausting but what helped me climb out of it was the idea that guilt was a way for my brain to deal with the situation. Guilt, whilst detrimental to your feeling of self-worth, makes you feel like you have some kind of control. Guilt was giving me a power I didn't have, whilst also shielding me from the cold truth that callous people will ignore your boundaries and there's nothing you can do about it.

This guilt mechanism is often seen amongst victims of child abuse. Children grow up believing they were to blame for their abuse, which is a slightly easier concept to process than the fact that people who are meant to protect you set out to hurt you. How can your young brain process something like that?

7. COMMUNITIES CAN HELP

What's helped me immensely in accepting my mental health issues is talking to other people with similar experiences. The same can be said after you've experienced sexual assault. In a support group you get to see how other people are carrying the same baggage as you. You might also be able to contextualise some of the emotions you're struggling with by seeing other people grapple with them. Trauma is incredibly isolating but getting together with other people can turn the table on your shame. In a group setting I feel a flicker of power in my belly: 'Look at us, we're sitting here, persisting, living our fucking lives despite the horrible things we've been through.'

8. DISSOCIATION IS SCARY BUT IT'S NOT UNUSUAL

I already talked a bit about dissociation. which is the sensation of being disconnected from either the world around you, yourself or both.

Dissociation during a traumatic event happens frequently. Psychiatrist Bessel van der Kolk writes in *The Body Keeps the Score*: 'Dissociation is the essence of trauma. The overwhelming experience is split off and fragmented, so that emotions, sounds, images, thoughts and physical sensations related to the trauma take on a life of their own.'

This fragmentation can occur at any point, during or after. I often feel like there's no way of knowing what might trigger it for me, even now, long after that evening. I might be in a pub having a Sunday roast when all of a sudden the back of my brain becomes a wardrobe I get sucked into. The other side isn't Narnia, it's a no man's land of white noise.

Whilst these episodes are scary what helped for me was normalising what was happening and trying my hardest not to fight it. If I could feel that floaty feeling set in I'd try and talk to myself with compassion: 'Something is triggering this. You feel unsafe. Remind yourself you're OK. You're doing fine.'

I began to see my dissociative episodes as my brain trying to integrate my experience. I started to view my mind and body as one, rather than two conflicting entities. They want to co-exist, they want to deal with what's happened to me, but they just struggle sometimes.

It was also helpful to stop trying to come up with a solution for everything that was happening. I'm one of those people who will run to Google whenever any kind of symptom occurs: 'Why is my eye twitching and what can I do to stop it?' After trauma your mind is completely shattered, it needs time to heal. Not everything that happens to you has a solution. Sometimes your mind just needs a little rest. When you sprain your ankle your body decides that it won't let you walk on that ankle. It hurts because it wants a break; the pain is functional. In a similar way, my dissociation is functional too. It's telling me to give my mind a rest. Don't push it. Don't push myself. Take things one step at a time.

9. NOT EVERYTHING YOU'LL DO TO COPE WILL BE GOOD FOR YOU

As a self-harmer it made sense to me to self-harm after the assault. My self-harm was performing a function. I'd been using it as a coping mechanism for over half my life, why wouldn't I use it now? Yes, it's unhealthy and damaging but now just wasn't the time to come up with a new plan. I had to resort to what I knew. I had to find some relief.

I also sought out sexual situations that weren't always right for me; I was trying to regain control by testing my limits. Perhaps part of me wanted to find out if all men were assholes. My body became a litmus test. If they stop when I tell them to then they're OK.

10. PEOPLE WITH GOOD INTENTIONS MAY STILL SAY THE WRONG THING

On top of managing your own feelings, should you wish to tell people about what happened to you, you may have to manage theirs as well. Some of the most hurtful comments might be voiced by those who love you the most. People say things that subtly slut-shame you or place the blame on you without meaning to. Even just a simple, 'Please be careful next time' implies that it was somehow your fault to begin with.

I think it's helpful to remember that people carry their own baggage with them wherever they go. When you share a story they'll interpret it through the filter of their own experiences and sometimes their response won't come out the right way.

Sometimes I fear that my boundaries are non-negotiable, that I'll never learn to trust someone or let my guard down, but then I remember that they aren't physical things. They're not actual walls, they *can* become flexible and prone to change if you want them to and you're ready. Your boundaries can extend and pull back as much as you're comfortable with. They're there to keep others at a safe distance but they allow you to choose who to let into the space you might exclude others from. You're in control and you can change your mind whenever you want. Your boundaries are yours.

10

REMEMBER THiS
WhEN YOU'RE LOSiNG
YOUR jOB

Keeping everything locked inside, hidden from view is a bad idea. I've known that since I was a kid. When I was bullied I'd swallow all the rage inside me, shut myself in my room and just sit there. The rage had nowhere to go. I hated those kids but I didn't do anything about it. I stored all that anger inside me until it began to turn on me: 'This is your fault. They're right. You *are* dumb. You *are* fat.'

That penchant for silence and bottling things up has cropped up in my work life as well, when the tasks keep piling up and everyone assumes I'm doing fine because I sit at my desk every day and I smile and say 'Hi' to people who walk past. In actual fact I've probably woken up that morning with EXTREME dread in my chest. I don't want to be at work. I don't think I can do it. I'm not cut out for this. I try and break my job down into little sections but when it comes to lunch I can hear people talking but nothing goes in. A manager might check in on me and I say, 'I'm fine', but meanwhile I feel like the room is spinning and I'm pretty sure my manager's head is slowly drifting off of her body. Things are really not fine.

One morning when I worked as a social media editor at BuzzFeed I'd reached a new limit. My levels of stress and exhaustion hit the summit. Instead of asking for help, calling in sick, seeing the doctor or even picking myself up and getting through the day, my mind and my body said, 'Enough!' They were finally working together, but not to my benefit.

I woke up and it was obvious: I wasn't going to go to work. I couldn't. I couldn't see the point. In fact I couldn't see the point in blinking, breathing or thinking. Nothing worked.

I lay on top of my duvet and tried to will dying on myself. I was too zombified to go out and kill myself but I wished for a secret power where I could shut my eyes and put a full stop on it all. What seemed like a few minutes of lying there, turned into hours. I hadn't moved. In my head time was passing in slow motion but in the real world things were ticking along as usual. My managers at work were naturally extremely worried.

In fact, they'd even called the police to show up at my house. My family had been called. My ex-boyfriends. In the space of me lying in bed trying to hold my breath I'd caused complete and utter chaos around me. Around 3pm that day I took a deep breath and pushed my upper body upright to check my phone. By then it was too late. I couldn't go into work. I had well and truly fucked up.

As you might imagine, the aftermath wasn't good. Instead of using this opportunity to be honest I opted for the usual: silence and sugar-coating. I blamed food poisoning and extreme tiredness. No one believed me. I told lie on top of lie and caused far more damage than I had to begin with.

When I told my BuzzFeed managers after things escalated and become much worse that I'd been suicidal for the past month naturally I was super distressed. I couldn't speak without crying. My skin was red and blotchy. My hands were shaking. I'd made a list of things to say when I approached them but I couldn't read the letters through my tears. It's easy to think, 'Oh only if I'd told them about this sooner', but at the time I was very much in the present, it was happening and I felt trapped. They told me I could go on an early lunch break, which I took eagerly and walked around Soho hoping to find something that would tell me what to do. My work building loomed in the background. I'd have to return at some point. I lit a cigarette and went to press it against my skin but stopped before it made contact. I couldn't do this again. My scars had just healed. I'd only just stopped wearing my bandages. My cigarette hung suspended in mid-air. A group of beauticians came out on their own smoke break and I moved somewhere quieter. I couldn't stop thinking about harming myself. Every item on the street looked like a tool I could use: a piece of glass, a window I could smash, a bus I could jump in front of. My mind went into video game mode spotting ways to cause damage.

I took a breath and let a different part of my brain take over. It was a softer part, gentler, it was looking out for me. I still seemed to be in a video game but in a different level altogether. This wasn't about hurting myself any more, I needed to get help. I needed to get to A&E. I texted work that I couldn't come back and went into A&E, using a voice that seemed to come from some alien part of my body that I was worried I was going to hurt myself. That I'd been seen here before for self-harm wounds and that I didn't think I was safe in my own company.

I felt like I wasn't me anymore. I was just a hollow bit of flesh, handing myself over to someone else's care. They looked after me, transferred me to a mental health unit and released me in the evening. There weren't any beds available and I managed to convince them I was going to be OK. I had a friend's house I could stay in. I'd see my counsellor the next day and to be honest, at this point, I was just too tired to do anything self-destructive.

The following week I came back to work carrying a massive load of shame with me. Thanks to the support of a few colleagues who were aware of my mental health issues I decided to finally tell the truth. I hadn't been doing well, I hadn't been looking after myself and my mental health was faltering. I wasn't fired but I was given an official warning and, in what ended up being a great result, my employers took some steps to make sure that not just mine but other people's mental health would be better supported in the office.

I should've felt relieved that I still had a job but I still was so desperately ashamed. Going into work was even harder than it had been before. I felt marked. I felt like I'd let everyone down. Then, to my surprise, a more senior colleague took me to lunch. He's a very clever and talented writer and editor I'd always looked up to. He had dark hair, a beard and always carried a fancy umbrella and a book that I'd scribble down in secret to make sure I read it too. I knew that he ran (and continues to run) a support group for people with bipolar disorder who work in the media. I'd vaguely spoken to him in the pub once about my issues and I think he saw straight in between the lines of my deflections and jokes that maybe I needed help. When I'd come back to work after a few days of absence he asked if I was free.

We went to a Korean restaurant near Oxford Circus. I tried to be happy and grateful that someone so senior wanted to spend his lunch with me. I wanted to ask him about some of the features he'd edited, career highlights, etc. I didn't want to talk about my fuck-ups, I didn't want to launch into some kind of dramatic monologue about how much I'd messed my career up but I took one bite of my kimchi and blurted everything out. He listened and said two things that I'll never, ever forget:

1. It's just a job.
   'Yes you fucked up,' he said, 'but ultimately it's just a job. You can find a new one.' I know this seems bizarrely simple but so much of my identity was tied up into this role and making it work – without it I didn't know who I was. If I was fired how would I pay my rent? How would I eat? What else could I possibly do?
2. You need to become your own advocate. 'You have to be your own carer, because if you don't do it, no one else will.'

When you have a mental illness that impacts your daily life you not only have to deal with the fallout from that but you also have to be there to clean it up, to defend yourself, to tell everyone this is not your fault. When you need support you have to go out there and get the help you need. You have to call various mental health services, you have to get yourself an appointment. If they're fully booked, don't give up. Ring someone else. Try another service. You have to keep going. It's important. I knew this but part of me was waiting for someone else to save me. Someone who'd swoop in and do all the calling and organising for me but at that point I'd alienated so many people it was really just me, by myself. I had to get myself better.

From that lunch on I tried to be better at being my own advocate. If I needed a day off from work because depression was crushing my skull I'd ask for it. If I needed to see my GP again to up my Citalopram dosage I'd give them a ring, and another ring if they were busy. I arranged to have another psych assessment as the others were inconclusive, which was a massive ball-ache to reschedule. I did it anyway. I had to.

When you're starting out in your job it's so hard to figure out how much you should disclose about your mental health. The bottom line for me has always been, considering the job market is a bit of a shit show, I've always been grateful to even have a job, and I'd rather not fuck it up.

Bad mental health isn't 'fucking up' though. A lot of conditions are protected from work discrimination under the Disabilities Act. The Act isn't there to tell you you're not normal, or good enough to join the team.

It's there to protect you when you're afraid your mental health is costing you your career.

There's a societal failure at present in adjusting for mental illness at work. Whereas in the past I've had no issue calling up because I have the flu, I've dragged my depressed body to work a number of times. It was only when I became honest about my situation that I was able to manage my work balance far better. I made a list of what I needed from work, which wasn't a lot. I needed to leave early on Wednesdays to make it to therapy and I needed to work from home on occasion if my anxiety or OCD flared up. The more specific about your requests, and why you're making them, the better. For example, my medication can make me feel quite groggy so working 10 till 6 is better for me than 9 till 5 as I can make sure my brain is alert before I start the day. I've worked in big open plan offices that would give the most rational person a dose of anxiety so I like the freedom of being able to move to a quieter room (usually an empty meeting room) so the noise doesn't make my brain whizz around.

Some workplaces are easier to ask for these adjustments than others. When I joined the BBC I was amazed at all the flyers and posters advertising mental health support and helplines and people you could talk to. It made approaching my own managers that much easier. I know there are bosses out there, and

I've experienced them, who belittle your condition, make you feel like you're a burden to the company and might even flat out refuse to give you any of the accommodation you need. It's so easy to say, dude, just quit! You don't need to work for those people. Thing is, not everyone has the privilege to just walk out of their job. You often have to sit there, grin and bear it and hope you can muster enough energy when you get home to put in a job application somewhere else.

There are things in place to support you, whether it's a union or a national mental health charity. Don't let your workplace make you even more miserable and make use of the facilities that are out there. You are not being an inconvenience.

It's up to you when you decide to tell your employer about any of your conditions, but from my experience the earlier on the better. If you wait till you're in the midst of something and crisis has struck you might not be as articulate as you'd like. Things might get emotional and complicated. There's also a chance your employers will feel misled: 'Why didn't she tell us about this before?'

Then, of course, there is the off-chance that despite all the precautions you have in place something boils up and BOOM you can't sit through a single meeting without welling up – whether it's your mental health or your situation sometimes you need to be able to let loose.

Here's how I've dealt with secret breakdowns at work:

- Go outside and stomp around the building. Go without a coat so you feel the cold. Scream into the wind

- Don't apologise if you're crying; you're allowed to cry and be emotional, there's nothing wrong with that.

- Go to the loo (hopefully your toilets have doors that go down to the ground else this might be a bit awkward), go into the foetal position on the floor, pop a hoodie over your face and just pretend you're somewhere else for a bit

- Punch the air really fast. Clench your fists and keep punching

- Arrange something fun to do after work so you know the second time is up you can bust out of there and do something more interesting

- Google other jobs (on the sly) that you can either apply for later or just to remind yourself that a job is just a job and you can get another one, it's fine

- Walk back to your desk and put your headphones on. Play 'I Will Survive' and get back to whatever it was you were doing for the remainder of the day

- Come in the next day dressed as a fucking queen, power suit and all

REMEMBER THiS
WhEN YOU'RE ALONe

When work and the wider world get too overwhelming I seek my own company more than
anyone else's. I see solitude as a warm bath. I love it.
I love sitting in it for hours, enjoying the warm water
enveloping my entire body. Only thing is, despite how
much I love it when I'm in it, I struggle with the idea of
it. A bath is just a stew of your own filth. Solitude is just
you and your own filth because no one else wants in.

There are different shades of aloneness. It's not as
simple as occupying a space without anyone else. It's
multi-layered and complex. I might have the house to
myself for the week, enjoying the comfort of being a
slob, not tidying up, singing out loud and then there's

a point when the loneliness piles up like a stack of dirty dishes. The stack gets higher and higher until it topples over and my room is littered with sad bits of ceramic.

There are types of isolation that make me feel uncomfortable. They are a different shade, darker, heavier and more restrictive. There's a self-imposed loneliness that's often a form of self-protection. People tend to experience this after a loss, whether it's a break-up or a loved one passing. In the midst of your grief, human contact seems unbearable. You put yourself in an isolation cell of your own making. It feels easier because the outside world operates at a different pace. They're not experiencing what you are, they are lost to you. No matter how many people offer to hold your hand, you're still achingly alone. You can't pass your grief around like a cigarette. It's yours to get through.

It's important to give yourself space whilst also giving yourself permission to be happy again because loneliness as a form of self-punishment is dangerous. You fold in on yourself. When I was a student, I banished myself to the confines of my flat. I exiled myself from the student union, the pubs and societies because I didn't think anyone would like me. Why would they? I was boring, dumb, lifeless. Why should I subject anyone else to that? I retreated so far into my exile that when a flicker of hope of genuine friendship arose I didn't make any effort. It was so much easier to give into the voices and agree, 'Yeah they'll probably just hate me anyway' than to follow up and actually take a chance.

There was also an anxiety that befriending someone would tie me into a binding contract. What if they wanted me to meet up all the time? What if they wanted me to go clubbing or do drugs? What if they wanted to stay over? What if I couldn't live up to their expectations? What if they never left me alone? It's incredibly frustrating when you've mentally entangled yourself to such an extent that such a simple thing as friendship seems like a bad idea. Why make the effort? Just go back to bed. Things are easier there.

Depression and anxiety often carry with them a loneliness that cages you in; you're landlocked with no place to go. It's a loneliness that's never subtle or passive. Instead it snaps at you, barks and chomps at your feet wherever you go. Even if you're in the middle of a crowd or surrounded by people who care about you, you still feel totally cut off. That feeling can be so visceral for me that I actually feel as if I'm taking up less space. I'm slowly disappearing. Everyone else's connectedness seems to mock how hollow my life feels. I hear teenage girls gossiping on the Tube and feel jealous. I see bartenders sharing a joke before a shift and wish I could join in. Why don't I have that? Why am I not bonded to anyone?

Another type of loneliness I experienced growing up stemmed from the fact that some of my most meaningful relationships were happening online. At fourteen I shied away from real friends and turned to friends I found on forums, where often quite self-destructive people came together to share details of their lives (more on these forums later).

To me these friendships were as real as the flesh-and-blood variety. We shared intimate details of our lives; what we'd had to eat, what music we listened to, who we were annoyed with that day. We shared lyrics and poetry and offered help and advice when we could. For me, these relationships added an element to my life that wasn't there: people to check in with. However, it took away the chance for me to build these connections in the real world – in school for example. My social skills faltered as I continually ran home to go on my computer and talk to women who were ten years older than me living far, far away. If I couldn't wait till then I'd go to the library at lunch and log in on the computers there.

I don't have these online friendships any more. I deleted my forum accounts when I was twenty. The pull of cyber companionship never waned but it was more important for me to build a life outside of my computer screen. Forums gave me an excuse to disengage from reality. I'll never be someone with a massive group of friends, but I have wonderful people in my life I love to see one-on-one. I share things with them, I confide in them and they help me grow as a person.

For me, loneliness requires a balancing act. It's not all doom and gloom. As an introvert I crave the space to fill my head with my own thoughts. I enjoy thinking out loud. I enjoy talking out loud. I enjoy not having to communicate with anyone else. What keeps solitude at a level I'm comfortable with is that I know, should I wish to go back to the 'real world', I have the option to engage with someone. Whether it's via phone or in person. My loneliness won't swallow me up. There's an expiry date. There's someone on the other end of the phone.

My optimum type of aloneness comes with a bit of preparation. Ideally, I want my room tidy, there has to be enough coffee in the house, I have taken off all my make-up, and my sheets are fresh and clean. I'm not wallowing in a crusty duvet wearing ketchup-stained pyjamas. I'm bundling myself up like a new baby. Everything feels clean and new and I get to enjoy it all by myself.

I also like knowing exactly what I'm going to do with alone time. It's not extended out in front of me like an African desert. I can visualise what I want to do, what I want to read and listen to. These activities can be unproductive. They'll probably include finding new golden retriever Instagram accounts to follow or making

163

a spreadsheet of shoes I'd like to buy once I'm rich. I try not to judge myself when I'm alone.

I like to make sure I eat and drink enough and I'm not surrounded by self-harm tools. It's important I make sure my solitude doesn't become an act of self-destruction like it used to be when my parents were away for the weekend. I'd use that time like I was an evil professor, inflicting experiments on my body. I'd try and see how long I could last without food or how much Bombay Sapphire I could drink without puking.

When I'm presented with a stretch of alone time now that seductive self-destructive whisper still creeps in. When my housemates say they're out of town or my boyfriend has plans in the evening my first instinct is: 'You can smoke your lungs out, you can cut yourself and you can drink at least two bottles of wine.' I have to reign these urges in. I can't use this time to 'get away' with anything. Other people aren't my enemies. I'm my own enemy. And every day I'm still proving that I can take care of myself. That I can use my 'me time' as an opportunity to be healthy and happy rather than miserable and reclusive.

I don't meditate when I'm alone but I'll engage in activities that feel like meditation to me: doodling, glueing things into my scrapbook, organising my books, planning hikes, using my analogue camera. As an introvert I find I recharge my batteries by being away from others. After Christmas or any other busy social occasion I'll need a 'me day' where I don't communicate with anyone but myself. I can feel a foamy wash cleanse my brain. I'm washing away the stress that comes with constantly being around people. I feel relaxed, my joints soften, my muscles ache less. I'm regenerating.

When I'm alone, I have the space to structure my thoughts like I'm reassembling a stack of fallen Jenga pieces. It allows me to reconnect my body and my brain and tune back in to my 'gut feeling'. When I'm in a group, I often fall into the part of people-pleaser, going along with whatever the rest want to do. I don't particularly mind this, it just means my own instincts are pushed further back until I can't actually hear them at all.

Being alone forces me to listen to my mind and my body. It forces me to stop and check in with myself. There's no one else to please apart from me.

Alone at home is one thing, then there's being alone in motion, when you're out and about or en route to somewhere. There aren't any clean sheets I can swaddle myself in but I enjoy it all the same. I like wandering by myself with a vague sense of purpose, towards an end goal that doesn't have a timed deadline: maybe a park or an exhibition. I try to walk at a slower pace when I'm doing this, not that fast trot I do when I'm rushing to work and my bags are flailing around the place.

When you're at a place where you're comfortable

with your own company I highly recommend taking yourself on a date. It's something people are constantly recommending in women's magazines and it feels cheesy, but I really do recommend it. A cinema is easy – you can hide in the darkness. A fancy meal can be trickier, but it's equally fulfilling. I like my own company in a restaurant. I like thinking about things, slowly, unhurried. I like ordering just for me. I like not having to come up with things to talk about and I like not having to worry if someone reaches for their phone. My social tics and stresses are shushed. I'm there for myself, with myself. There's no pressure.

I've taken myself to lots of different places: McDonald's, fancy French restaurants, diners, service station cafes, cosmopolitan bars, Mars-themed sports bars, Dutch bars abroad – most bars to be honest.

Whether, like me, you'd like to have a great date in McDonald's or you're thinking of something a little more upmarket here are some things you might find useful:

- Don't worry about anyone staring at you. On the whole, people are too wrapped up in their own lives to notice other people. Even when I have spotted someone eating alone I never thought they were lame or sad, if anything I was envious
- If being seen is still a worry for you, you can go for a table in the corner rather than bang in the

middle of the room. I like sitting by the window so I can look out at the world and I don't feel too enclosed

- Bring a book or a newspaper, or another form of entertainment. There's no one on your table telling you you're being rude. I once saw a guy in Pizza Express eating on his own whilst he kicked back with a glass of wine, some dough balls and an episode of *The Wire* on his laptop. Goals

- Bring a notepad. When I eat alone I like to make notes. These aren't super profound Aristotelian observations but they might be little descriptions of people or some material for poetry or a short story I'll get to later. It's nice to give myself the space to sit, enjoy food someone else has made and be creative

- Eavesdrop as much as you like. It's possibly the best perk about eating alone: listening to other people's conversations. You might hear an awkward first date, co-workers gossiping about their boss or two old friends making amends after a fall-out

- Next to eavesdropping you can people-watch as much as you like. Where I'm from in the Netherlands it's all about terrace life. Most bars and restaurants have an outside section where the chairs face the street. You're all gazing in the same direction, watching people walking and cycling past. If you can, opt for a terrace, sit there for hours

- Pay attention to what you're eating. Order things that are bursting with flavour: rich pasta sauces, bitter coffee, velvety red wine. Roll the ingredients round your tongue, dig your teeth in and relish in the food you've treated yourself to

- Don't feel like you have to chat to anyone. The best thing for me about bars in the UK is that bartenders rarely strike up a conversation. At most, they'll ask what I'm reading or whether I want another drink. When I went to New York by myself I did a lot of sitting at a bar with a book and the bartenders would not stop chatting. Some of them were dashing and charming and had relatively interesting stories to tell, others would fill me in on their fantasy football league or pass judgement on my choice of drink. I've learnt to be quite cut-throat if someone is talking to me and I'm not in the mood. It's perfectly OK to put your head back down and delve back into your book. I've been overly polite for most of my life; it's time to let a few things go. If I'm reading and you're

    telling me my choice of white wine is unrefined
    you can piss off

● If you're not comfortable taking yourself out to
    a restaurant just yet, start with smaller activities
    and then build on them. Go further away from
    home, go for longer and eventually, when you're
    ready, go on an adventure

At a point where my mental health was teetering over the edge of 'Houston we have a problem', I decided to take myself out of London. I found an extraordinarily cheap Eurostar ticket and a tiny Airbnb studio I could stay in for 20 euros a night right by Père Lachaise. Unfortunately, my timing wasn't great. My Eurostar from London to Paris left on the morning after the Brexit referendum. I'd been up all night refreshing the *Guardian* live blog, not really leaving any space in my brain to think about the possibility that Leave votes would hold the majority. The moment the results were announced I felt my stomach sink but I had no time to despair. I had an hour to get to St Pancras to board my train.

This was supposed to be the beginning of a chapter – a new me – but I felt depleted. I'd come to the UK five years ago to study and build a life. I'd immersed myself in Cornish pasties, *EastEnders* and dunking biscuits into tea, but the country I'd chosen to make a home in didn't want me anymore. Britain was breaking up with me.

Rationally, I knew I couldn't take this personally, and I shouldn't make it all about me, but my crutches were being kicked out from underneath me. I was losing my relationships, friendships and job, but at least I felt like I was living in a country that was my home. I retweeted tweet upon tweet that agreed with my feelings, but it was like trying to scratch an itch I could never reach. I wanted to speak to someone, to share my emotions, but the rest of the Eurostar passengers were chatting about the vote like it was something that happened somewhere else. I slouched down in my seat and tried to sleep.

When we passed Brussels, a handsome man with hazel eyes and strong arms you could build a home in sat in the empty seat next to me. I'd wanted this trip so much to end up all *Before Sunrise*. I was a sassy yet studious young woman who would meet an intellectually intriguing man on the train and we'd engage in a whirlwind trip of European cities (or in my case we could just go to Paris). My new train neighbour would be my ticket to my own Richard Linklater trilogy. I wanted it so badly. I sat up straighter and made sure there was no drool crusting up the corner of my mouth. My own private Ethan Hawke smiled at me. My heart leapt. It's happening. He then leant into his bag and took out a newspaper. A massive Brexit headline greeted me and my enthusiasm popped on the spot. What's the point? The world is broken I silently declared, I'll pass on romance today.

I went back to sleep and woke up in Paris. When I walked out of Gare du Nord I was drunk from tiredness and starting to get increasingly annoyed with myself. I realised I'd forgotten to buy socks or deodorant. My phone was refusing to connect to any Wi-Fi zones and I couldn't afford to buy any more data. There was no way of finding out how to get to my Airbnb because I hadn't written down the address.

I tried three different cafes and just when I thought I should give up and go back to the UK, my phone connected to a Wi-Fi network. I sat down and ordered two cappuccinos whilst retrieving my Airbnb info. I wasn't too far from the studio. I was doing OK. 'You got this,' I told myself, like a reluctant cheerleader. 'You can travel alone.'

The host had left a key under the mat so I let myself into his small apartment. The space was tiny but it had everything a person would need: a stove, bathroom, table, chair and a fold-out bed. I'd been slightly disappointed not to meet the host, it made me feel like a ghost in his residence. I wanted to have a conversation with someone before committing to the next three days of not speaking to anyone at all.

I set to work on the fold-out bed and enjoyed a brief

but restorative nap. I woke up and remembered I was in Paris. I couldn't let this go to waste. I hopped on the Metro to Montmartre and walked around looking for a coffee shop that wasn't too busy. I drank three cappuccinos and smoked outside until I felt awake enough to keep walking. I went to the Sacré-Coeur where an exhausted father carrying three children like sacks of potatoes asked me if it was worth getting a ticket: 'Is it any good in there?' I lied and said no because it felt like both him and his kids needed a break.

On my way back to the studio I found a restaurant a friend had recommended but it looked too trendy for me to eat in by myself. At that point I wasn't as comfortable with solo dining as I am now. Everyone looked well dressed and interesting and head over heels with whoever they were talking to. I went to a restaurant next door that seemed less hip and more cosy. I ordered a salad because it's the only thing I could decipher from the menu.

I soon realised what makes eating alone even stranger in a foreign country: you can't eavesdrop on anyone. It's like you're in a bubble, there's no verbal link between you and your surroundings. I gave up on trying to understand French and committed to my book whilst shovelling salad leaves into my mouth.

I walked the remaining hour and a half to the studio. En route I bought wine, more cigarettes and three Kinder eggs. I drank most of the wine in transit and finished the bottle off when I collapsed on the dinky fold-out bed. I felt good but empty; tears were starting to appear in the fabric of my new solitude and it had only been one day.

I opened my laptop and scrolled through Facebook but my tipsy vision wasn't allowing any words to sink in. In the corner of my screen I saw my ex was online, the little green circle giving him away. It had been a month since we broke up and we had only talked to each other about our flat situation and who was responsible for the last instalment of rent. It was a messy, circular fight that meant there was no room for us to actually ask if the other person was doing OK. It was all business.

Spurred on by all the supermarket wine swimming in my belly I typed a 'Hi' and waited. Facebook told me he was typing back but nothing showed up in the box. 'He's thinking about it though, this is good!' I thought naively.

'Sorry if this is a bad time. Just wanted to see how you were doing?' I hastily typed, before he'd give up typing and I'd lose him forever.

He said he was doing fine and he returned the question. 'I'm OK,' I replied, 'I'm in Paris, just getting away from it all.' He responded, 'Please take care of yourself,' which seemed more like an order than a sign of compassion. He knew about my struggles with self-harm and seeing as we were both in a bad place knowing I was completely alone in another country couldn't have been a very comforting thought. I also got the overwhelming feeling that he wanted this conversation to end, but I was too drunk and desperate to stop. Instead of calling it a night I poured what had been happening to me recently into the little chat box: 'Hey erm, this feels like a weird thing to say, but it's not like we'll ever meet up again. They, as in various doctor people, think I might be bipolar.'

Silence, then: 'Ah OK, wow.'

I went into it a little more, explaining how my erratic behaviour towards the end of our relationship might have been more than me being a knob. There may be some faulty wires in my brain chemistry. Perhaps there was something to salvage? Perhaps our relationship could be saved?

The next chunk of messages read like me chucking pasta at a wall hoping some of it would stick. I was desperate to keep him engaged. I couldn't have him leave, despite the fact that he was only responding with stoic one-word answers. Eventually he said he had to go and I signed off with: 'I didn't mean to inconvenience you, you should go live your life.'

I shut my laptop aggressively and stared ahead of me at a patch of mould that seemed to take on the shape of my own face. How had I been this pathetic? I was a nuisance to my ex. I'd annoyed him. I'd imposed my mental health issues on him. Just because I didn't have anyone else to talk to didn't mean I had to force him to be on the receiving end. I'd fucked up and felt my eyes well up. Loneliness crept in accompanied by an acute sense of failure. I had turned the one person I felt safest with against me and now I was crying in a kitchen-slash-living-room-slash-square-box where no one would care. What a waste of time and money.

My self-pity eventually lullabied me to sleep. When I woke up, my head throbbed, my eyes were twitching and the weight of my failed conversation descended on me like an avalanche. 'I can't do this,' I thought, 'going outside today is just too hard.' I felt undeserving of Paris. It was so beautiful and here I was in it, hungover, smelly and sad. I shut my eyes hoping I'd feel better after another quick snooze but when I opened them I'd been asleep for another seven hours. Fuck. I'd essentially wasted an entire day.

My phone flashed and my sister sent me a picture of our favourite French actor, Louis Garrel, accompanied by the question of whether or not I'd met a handsome French man yet. I told her I wasn't having a great time, that I'd massively overslept and stupidly drunk Facebooked my ex and it all went to shit. She responded, 'NOOOOO!' followed by, 'Give me your address.' She fired back with three bars in my area I should check out. I didn't want to but her all-caps ambush was bizarrely motivational.

She was right, after all. I still had some time of my day left. What else was I going to do? I chose the bar that was nearest and headed out, after I had showered mascara trails off my cheeks.

The bar was slightly too hip and happening for my liking. I chose a bar stool as I silently cursed my sister for forcing me to go here. There was this impeccably glamorous woman at the bar, also sitting alone. She looked like she belonged in a French version of *Sex and the City*. I looked down at my hoodie, my Primark dress and dirty trainers and scolded myself for not making more of an effort. A handsome man in a tweed suit came up to her, they kissed passionately and sat at a table together. I felt like I'd lost a comrade, albeit a far superior one. I was the only solo woman now. I took out my book, ordered an apple cinnamon Martini and focused on the words on the page. I was so wrapped up in the story that when I looked up again I'd been there for a full hour and hadn't felt too weird. I was doing OK.

I walked home feeling accomplished and managed to get some sleep without firing off any more drunk Facebook messages. The next morning I updated my Spotify playlist and decided to set out on a wander with no real purpose. I walked and walked and only checked Google Maps about an hour in. I took photos. I ate a croissant and sang along to Fiona Apple in my earphones. I felt like I was in a movie but in a filler scene: this wasn't advancing the plot, I was simply just being.

When my legs began to ache I figured out my way

home going through the famous Père Lachaise cemetery. I'd been there before so I didn't get stressed out about having to find Oscar Wilde or Jim Morrison's tombstones. I was the most relaxed and the most present I'd felt in months. I'd given up on my frantic search for connection. I didn't feel lonely any more. I felt at peace, letting my body move in whichever direction it wanted to.

When I went back to Britain I still had a lot of shit to deal with, Brexit being one of them, but I kept up this new form of walking I'd learnt. Walking without a clear purpose has led me to discover beautiful places in London: marshes and hills and mews and lavender fields. And I've gone further afield. I've been hiking in Hastings and Essex and I've taken myself on romantic beach walks on the south coast. I've learnt that I'm not bad company; I'm all right and the more I can let go the better I am as a travel buddy. I've learnt to stop looking for a connection elsewhere and to start trying to connect the fragmented bits within myself.

Here's what I learnt on my solo excursions:

- Figure out your travelling style and commit to it. Whether I'm travelling alone or with someone I like to build an itinerary; I like to do my research before and I like to get excited about some of the things I'm going to see. My

old housemate Virginie is a keen solo traveller
but her style is totally different. She makes sure
she's packed enough clothes, has enough foreign
currency and one night of accommodation on the
day she arrives. She'll also allow herself to buy
one guidebook that she won't open until she's
on the plane travelling to her destination. This
is how she travels and she thrives doing it. She's
been to Nepal, Burma and Mexico and likes to
be surprised and steered by her own spontaneous
curiosity. It's the thing I love about her the most
but it's absolutely not for me

● Figure out what the things are that make you
stressed when travelling and plan ahead. Get
the visa and travel insurance sorted, and get
yourself a physical map in case you're like me
and your phone is constantly dying

● Don't be afraid to approach people. If you need to
ask for directions or you want to ask for a good
place to eat open your mouth and strike up a
conversation. Start small if you're nervous: maybe
ask a receptionist where the closest ATM is or ask
your Airbnb host where the best breakfast spot is

● If you want to be alone but not completely
alone you can meet other solo travellers by
staying in hostels, guesthouses or community-
run accommodation. You could even travel with

a small-group tour company that gives you the option to make friends

- There are lots of Facebook groups and online networks you can join for the area you'll be travelling to, which will help you suss out what you want to do when you get there (or even plan a meetup and make a friend)

- Schedule a regular check in with people back home. It's nice for them to know you're still alive and it's comforting knowing someone is keeping an eye out for you. If your friends and family tend to worry about you stick to a pre-arranged time, e.g. every other day at 7pm, so you don't have to faff around with finding a right time in different timezones or getting your phone to work whilst you're on top of a mountain

- This might sound a bit childish but it works for a lot of people. If you find yourself getting a bit stressed whilst you're off on your own somewhere it can help to start talking to yourself as 'we'. The other person can be an invisible partner, a friend or just another you. Using an imaginary 'we' gives you a sense of companionship and security. I often change between a 'we' and a 'you' – the 'you' comes from the other me that's cheering the actual me along. So when I made my train back from Paris when

I thought I was about to miss it I said (out loud even): 'Well done, you did it!'

● Don't feel like you have to say yes to everything. Even if you're embarking on your own version of *Eat Pray Love* and you want to experience everything you don't have to be spontaneous 24/7. You're allowed to say no to some things. If you want to have a nap, have that nap. If you want to go to McDonald's instead of a hyper-local street food cafe you're allowed to. Don't put pressure on yourself, trust your instincts and listen to your gut: what do you really want to do?

12

REMEMBER THiS
WhEN YOU'RE ONLiNE

One way to travel and explore without really having to leave your bed is to log onto your computer. Online you can witness sights and sounds and different people. It's easy to feel a sense of community. The internet can be a place where you can find a hub of support with wonderful people giving great advice, but it's also a hotbed of self-loathing, loud-mouthed trolls and self-destructive clubs.

I don't envy teens who grow up today, with the internet wrapped around wherever they go. I was teased in school. I hid in gym toilets and beneath staircases to get away from the chanting. The greatest escape would come when it was time to go home. There was no more invasion of words and pokes and trip ups; no one could get me when I was holed up in my room. Now with social media the bullying never stops. You go home, log on and it starts all over again. People have pictures and videos. It's impossible to feel safe.

Even if you don't have to deal with bullies the internet is filled with booby traps of upsetting content. There are articles, videos and images begging for your click. Even if a publication doesn't aim to cause you any harm, just reading about self-harm or seeing scars might ignite the urge within you. Eating disorder recovery stories in tabloids always get to me. The focus is never on how healthy the person is now, it's on how sick they once were. They splash images of bones and feeding tubes trying to shock you. It's less about the well-being of the person they're writing about and more about enticing the body horror fantasy within the reader.

I have to approach the internet with care. Every couple of days I fall into a YouTube hole where I have to text my boyfriend and he comes to my rescue – usually by taking the phone out of my hand. After a tough day recently I went to the pub and embarked on a three-hour YouTube expedition into videos about the Manson murders. As the pub grew darker I became less conscious of my surroundings, clicking on a new clip as soon as the current clip had ended. I was getting more and more upset. I felt horrified for the victims, the young women who had been indoctrinated by the cult, and even Charles Manson who'd experienced a childhood of rape and abuse.

When it was finally time to leave the pub I was drained, zombie-like and my eyes twitched from the hyperfocus strain I'd put on them. And this situation wasn't a one-off for me. The internet feels infinite — once I start reading up on troubling material I will keep going, even if it's upsetting me. Even if there's a big trigger warning splashed across something I'll click it, just to see what it is. 'It can't be that bad,' I'll think — and it always is.

Whilst I can't approach the internet with gloves on I can identify the places I know will hurt me mentally. The internet is vast but there are little patches I know I need to avoid. Here are some of them:

PRO-ANA COMMUNITIES

There's a dark, cult-like corner of the internet, which used to reside mostly on LiveJournal and Xanga, that attracts people from all over the world who seem intent on starving themselves.

Pro-ana (pro-anorexia) and pro-mia (pro-bulimia) are terms used by people who talk about eating disorders like they're a lifestyle choice instead of the crippling mental disorders they are. Members of pro-ana groups exchange tips, 'thin commandments' and 'thinspiration' to motivate one another to continue dieting, bingeing, and purging.

I first joined a pro-ana community when I was thirteen. I had been given a writing assignment about eating disorders and female representation in the media. Coincidentally, I was also given a drama assignment to create a five-minute play about bulimia.

Whilst I was doing research for these projects I read an article condemning pro-ana communities on Xanga and LiveJournal. The article said these forums were a threat to young girls and needed to be shut down. I had never heard of pro-ana before. I decided to stop reading about it and experience the whole thing myself. I made an account, gave myself a fake name and dove in.

Reading back my own LiveJournal entries, it doesn't feel like me. I was trying to copy the pro-ana mindset, own it, and eventually adopt it, which I did. Pro-ana women were angsty, angry and insecure, and I found comfort in that. That was how I felt on the inside, even before I hated my body.

Partaking in their challenges gave me a sense of purpose and control. There was a group where they'd set a calorie limit for the day and whoever stuck to it the most 'won'. You didn't win anything apart from admiration from your fellow group members, which for people who were social misfits in their real lives meant everything.

The first groups I joined had names like 'anaXcore' and 'proed_bones' and have since been deleted or changed into 'pro-recovery' communities. Membership required you to post stats and a brief history of your experience with bingeing and purging. For me, that was pretty hardcore. I lurked, almost admiring the dedication but not wanting to tell a stick-thin teenager that she should 'keep going'. Some group members would post naked photos of themselves and invite critique: 'You could probably do with losing some weight on your hips' or 'Your collarbones would look cute if they're more pronounced.' These comments were people's own eating disorders talking, and who could blame them? We live in a society where female bodies in particular are constantly scrutinised, even policed. These pro-ana members had perfected the art of scrutiny.

Whilst the pro-ana group offered me a refuge from my depression, isolation and aimlessness, it taught me how to be mean. Not to other people but to myself. My journal entries are endless streams of: 'I'm fucking ugly', 'I'm a bitch', 'I'm so fucking stupid.' I still have those voices today.

I did make friends on LiveJournal. There was a group of older women who took me in as their virtual younger sister. We stopped talking about food and dieting, and they helped me with my homework and introduced me to Sylvia Plath, Elliott Smith and Fiona Apple. I genuinely owe the discovery of a lot of the music and literature that shaped me to those women.

Unfortunately, though, those friendships didn't come without a cost. We could send each other songs but we couldn't save each other. I had to delete my account a few times as my mum or a boyfriend found them but I could never tell my online friends what had happened. We were constantly stressed when people didn't log on. Some women were absent because they had to go to rehab or they were sectioned. One woman I cared about greatly posted a final piece of writing about how she'd gone off the rails and descended back into her crystal meth addiction. I still think about that woman every day. I never knew her real name or where exactly she lived. I have no way of knowing if she's OK.

These types of communities come in all shapes and sizes. When I shared my pro-ana stories with my first housemate in London she told me she'd joined something similar as a teen but it was about self-harm. She told me you'd post photos of your cuts in forums, share tips on how to cut deeper and how to hide the wounds from your parents. She'd spent the same amount of time in those groups as I had in mine. I loved her and still think she's one of the most wonderful women I've ever met, but she doesn't know that herself and can't accept it. That dangerously cruel voice she honed on those sites, telling her she deserved all that self-inflicted pain, is still with her today, telling her she's worthless.

If you put a bunch of scared, lonely and self-destructive people together you can't expect them to be equipped with the right tools to help each other out.

TROLL COMMENTS

As an adult using the internet now, you might not have bullies you know personally attacking you online, but you still have to deal with trolls – people who sit in dark rooms spewing out their own personal agenda in comments and tweets, tearing anyone down who stands in their way.

A study by communications professor Stine Eckert concluded that 73.4 per cent of women who blog or post about feminism, family and/or maternity politics on their social media accounts receive abusive comments, stalking, trolls, rape threats, death threats and unpleasant offline encounters.

I once wrote an article with the sarcastic title of '21 Reasons You Should Never Visit the Netherlands'. It was a style of headline that BuzzFeed used a lot at the time. It drives people's curiosity and once they click they realise the page is filled with reasons the country is actually beautiful.

Simple, right? Well, I still get messages from people who never bothered to click. They send them to my Facebook, Twitter and my personal email. They tell me I'm a bitch, a whore, that it's good I don't live in Holland, that they should take away my passport, that I don't deserve my nationality. I used to reply asking them to actually read the damn thing but I've stopped now – there's no point.

The best way to deal with trolls is to ignore them, but that seems like you're backing down or hiding away. Platforms like Facebook and Twitter are flawed in that they're not very good at protecting their users from abuse, but it's still important to report people who send you things that make you feel unsafe.

GOOGLE

It's a bit unfair to claim that Google is bad for my mental health – on the whole it isn't, but it is incredibly easy to use Google to make my hypochondria thrive. From convincing myself I'm pregnant with a demon baby made of finger nails to thinking I have syphilis and meningitis at the same time, my Google searches send me into a pit of despair.

Whilst Google has helped me find solace in anxiety forums where people talk about their panic attacks and other symptoms, what became problematic was that reading about panic attacks tended to bring one on. I'd be trying to find comfort in other people's posts about how they too didn't get through their bus journey, but in reading about their shortness of breath, dizziness and hot flushes, my body seemed to mimic everything I was reading.

I think these forums are fantastic, but when you're still in a place where you're hypersensitive and you wear your triggers on your sleeve, you have to be careful you don't drown in a research avalanche.

When I was diagnosed with borderline personality disorder I felt very comfortable with my diagnosis. I'd been reading about it for years; I read scientific journals and psychology magazines and I have a great therapist who will point me in the right reading direction. However, when you Google a diagnosis with no prior knowledge of what it actually is you can get sucked into accusatory and inaccurate articles.

When my boyfriend told me he was reading up about my personality disorder I typed it into Google to see how the articles would look from his point of view. The third one Google suggested was an article called: 'Why You Should Never Date Girls with BPD'. Granted, the article was hosted on a meninist alt-right website, so I should've expected it really, but it was so hurtful to even see that title pop up. When you're using the internet in search for comfort you have to remember there are a lot of thorns in your way. Don't take everything you read seriously.

INSTAGRAM

There are so many great communities on Instagram – take the body positive movement for example. They exist solely to connect people, spread self-love and combat societal pressures. However, there's a part of Instagram that makes me feel inadequate, no matter how much my feed is filled with badass women, golden retrievers and toddlers dressed like superheroes.

In a recent UK Snapchat survey, Instagram was rated the worst social platform when it comes to young people's mental health. People aged 14–24 complained that the app caused a whole host of issues, including loneliness, depression, bullying and negative body image.

The platform thrives off people's cleverly curated lives and pushes those lives right into our feeds. My holiday will never look as good as someone else's holiday, and that someone else will always have the very thing I want, whether it's a stable relationship, purple hair or that new book everyone's raving about.

When I'm in a good place I use Instagram for inspiration. I'll save posts of fun places to eat in my neighbourhood or cheap European cities I want to explore. When I'm in a bad place Instagram is a gateway drug to self-doubt. I'll lurk on the profiles of three different ex-boyfriends, three women I think are intimidating, and sometimes I'll even trawl through my own profile judging it like I'm the Simon Cowell of social media.

There's another Instagram-related habit I have that is absolutely detrimental and perhaps the ultimate form of social media self-sabotage: the unfollower app. Three times a year I allow myself to download an app that tells me who has unfollowed me on Instagram. Every time I imagine it'll be a fun exercise: 'Oh look, that spambot unfollowed me' or 'Oh that blogger who probably thought I was more interesting unfollowed me' or 'My ex-boyfriend's mum has finally deleted me, ha ha ha.' Thing is, each time I've allowed myself to use this app there's always something that bothers me that little bit too much and I get caught in a spiral of self-hatred.

I once found out that a former manager of mine who I always looked up to as being a very cool, savvy woman with all the business smarts in the world had pressed the 'unfollow' button on my account. She still followed everyone else we'd both worked with (I double-checked), but I hadn't made the cut. I should have shrugged and moved on but I became mildly obsessed with this. I was tempted to phone her up to ask if she'd made a mistake (thank god I didn't follow through with this). I then looked at my account through the eyes of my friends and concluded there must be something terribly off-putting about my posts. Maybe I post too frequently? Maybe my captions are too rude? Maybe my filters are too garish?

I thought about deleting my account for a second until I stepped back and thought about how extreme my behaviour was at this point. It's a social media platform, it's not real life, chill out! I've now started to use Instagram in a healthier way.

I've unfollowed 'hate follows' (the people you actually dislike but you follow them to have a good sneak peak at their lives) and I've limited my lurking on people's profiles to twice a week (nobody's perfect). Here are some other ways I've made my account more mental health safe:

- Find your community: Instagram can be a friendly, supportive place if you surround yourself with the right people. If you have a hobby or a cause you particularly care about fill your feed with those followers. I'm part of a Facebook group for female writers in London and someone posted on their Instagram account wondering if people wanted to connect on there. I jumped in and added about 100 new people who were all similar to me: they loved books and writing and writing about books. My Instagram feed became less of a source of worry and more of inspiration and camaraderie

- You don't have to be brutally honest but don't feel like you have to make your account picture-perfect all the time. Unless your goal is to become an influencer with a gazillion followers

you can be relaxed about what you post.
Granted, I'm not comfortable posting a selfie of
me in A&E when I'm getting my second-degree
burns treated, but I might post a picture of a
crowded gig and how I was trying to ward off an
anxiety attack. Doing this, I've connected with
lots of other people who often post about
their anxiety and it helps us to be supportive
of each other

● Every now and again go on an Instagram detox.
Step back and do an audit of everyone you follow.
Does that friend who always bangs on about their
yoga routine make you feel lazy and useless?
Maybe get rid of them? You can also go into
your settings and ban certain words from your
comments in case you often get sucked into long
comment threads you'd rather not be part of

● Get a face-editing app. Seriously, once I got
myself the facetune app I realised how easy it is
to make your face look slimmer, more refined
and glowing. Even all those Snapchat filters that
give you dog ears also sneakily make you look
less pale. The reason everyone looks so banging
on Instagram is because they've added an effect
or two. I've never actually posted a facetuned
creation of mine, apart from the time I posted a
photo my sister took of me where my arms are

up and I blurred out a nasty shaving rash on my armpit. It didn't really work because I just ended up with a blurry pit, but still. It taught me that if you're skilled at certain apps you could use it to all sorts of effect. The more you realise how airbrushed a lot of your Instagram faves are, the more you can put it into perspective. They put a lot of effort into looking that hot. If you can be bothered, great, and if not: stop worrying about it. It's not real

INTERNET STALKING

Everyone looks up everyone else online. My first ever boyfriend and I became good friends after we broke up and he told me about a fight he was having with his new girlfriend. Apparently he'd seen that she checked my Instagram, Twitter, Facebook and poetry Tumblr (hope she enjoyed my lack of iambic pentameter) most mornings before she got out of bed. He told her to stop doing it, but it had become so routine for her she didn't want to give it up.

Instead of being a bit freaked out by this it actually made me want to run to her house to give her a massive hug and tell her I'd been stalking her just as much. I'd seen every inch of her life that existed online: from her Facebook page to her acting showreel to her vintage jewellery account on Etsy. There was nothing she'd put online that I hadn't seen. The fact that someone was doing that level of snooping to me, a totally boring average individual, seemed ridiculous. She deserved to be stalked. She was an actress, she had long ginger hair like a mermaid, she liked Kanye – she was PERFECT. I wanted to connect to her and say look it's OK, I'm not very interesting, stop wasting your mornings on my accounts. Go live your life! That's not how it works though. Instead we keep our heads down and convince ourselves that everyone else is better.

My Instagram snooping has become more arbitrary as time has gone on. It used to be the standard: ex-boyfriend's new girlfriend. You want to see if they've got something you weren't able to offer. It's not ideal, but we all do it. However, my snooping has branched out much further than that, and sometimes I even forget why I was on their account in the first place. For instance, I might stumble on my friend's godmum's very rich son-in-law. Boom. I'm hooked now, and I wake up thinking: 'What's Hugo up to lately? Does he have a new car? A new house? A new girlfriend?'

Whether you're dealing with trolls or bullies or your ex flaunting their new happy life, the internet is a mindfuck. For me, it's become incredibly important to treat the internet like a garden I've planted. I want the good things to grow and I want to get rid of the weeds. I've cultivated a place I feel safe. A place that makes me learn and a place that makes me laugh. Here's how:

- Engage with charities and organisations you care about. I found a charity that helps fight period poverty and they supply tampons and sanitary pads to female refugees who can't afford them. I started following them, and championing them online as much as possible

- Use your skills to do something useful. I started helping out with the social media feeds of a great charity in London who teach young women to play musical instruments. I spent time getting their word out there, designing assets and attracting influencers who could help out

- Find comfort in Facebook groups – so long as you don't find talking about mental health to be triggering. I'm part of twenty-five-and-counting Facebook groups. I love them. They make my Facebook usage more personal. Of those, ten are mental health groups, from 'Women with Anxiety' to 'Women on the Borderline' (you guessed it: a group for women with borderline personality disorder). You can use it to share some of the things you're struggling with or to celebrate the small everyday victories that people without mental health issues might not understand

- I also set up my own group called 'Women & Mental Health', where members share articles around mental health issues that either got it extremely right or extremely wrong and we engage in a friendly discussion about that

- Mental health communities on Twitter are great too. Twitter can feel like an endless stream of humblebrags or self-deprecation or both, but there are also lots of activists, spokespeople and those who are dedicated to breaking down stigma

- I post anonymously about my mental health struggles on subreddits on reddit. I've made some friends there and we now use a shared app so we can chat about our therapy, relationship issues and triggers on a daily basis

- Online support communities like Big White Wall and 7 Cups are great mental health resources too

13

REMEMBER THiS WhEN YOU'RE GETTING HeLP

- It's important you don't try and tackle your mental health issue by yourself – confide in someone. It can feel hard to talk about what's going on in your mind – it feels like you're oversharing or causing a scene or a fuss about nothing – but before you send yourself into a shame spiral keep these things in mind, because it's not at all weird to talk about mental health. Trust me
- At least 1 in 4 of us experience mental health issues
- By 2030, it is estimated that there will be approximately two million more adults in the UK with mental health problems than there were in 2013

- Young women are the most at risk; more than <u>one third</u> of young women in Britain have reported feeling unhappy or worthless
- Keeping your problems a secret makes it seem like it's your fault
- Keeping them a secret makes it seem like this type of thing is incredibly uncommon (it's not, hello – 1 in 4!)
- The world can't see inside your mind, you have to tell them about it
- Talking is the quickest way to show someone you're in pain
- No one should be made to feel like they have to hide any part of themselves
- Asking for help is important
- Asking for help might save your life
- You wouldn't find it strange to talk about a broken leg, so why should a broken brain be any different?
- Mentally ill people are not A DANGER TO SOCIETY as many headlines, TV shows and films will have you believe
- Talking can be a lot like slowly letting air out of a balloon that's about to burst inside of you
- Friendships will grow stronger the more honest you are
- Relationships will never work if you shut yourself off

REMEMBER THiS WhEN YOU'RE SaD

- ● The people who judge mental health conditions are the people you don't want around you anyway
- ● In sharing your struggles you're letting someone know they can come to you if they find themselves in a similar position
- ● Being vulnerable can make you stronger

When I was eight, I formed a band at school called The Georgie Kids. Our school was St George's School, so it wasn't the most inventive band name in the world. However, I *did* write an award-winning song (we won 'Most Enthusiastic' in the winter talent show) called 'Friendship for a Lifetime'. The song is catchy in that it just repeats: 'Friendship for a lifetime, we sing it daytime and night-time' over and over and over again until you want to bang your head against a wall.

The one and only song I've ever written shows how I've always yearned for close friendships. I wanted to be in a gang, a group or, best case scenario, a badass girl squad. Because I moved schools over and over again thanks to my dad's job, I never assembled that solid gathering of friends. Even now, I have people I love more than anything dotted around different countries. Some I see weekly, some I see hardly at all.

I learnt that there's no blueprint to friendship. Every-one has different needs and expectations. At least by never belonging to a big group of people I've never experienced the negative sides either: the falling outs and other dramas. Perhaps a group would never have suited me anyway. Maybe I would fade into the background or constantly go along with whatever everyone else wants to do?

I have been on one large group holiday; it was at the end of school and it was our senior year trip. Whilst people split off into groups to go to foam parties and drink bowls of supermarket-brand cola with a few drops of rum, I felt a bit intimidated by all the bright lights and loud music that emanated from the nightclubs. I have come to realise I am pretty much a dog, I just want to lie on the floor and have my back stroked. Don't make me go into an overcrowded box where my feet stick to the floor.

Instead of forcing myself to join the hordes of school chums on the dance floor, I went to bed and got up at 7am the next day to go to an archaeological site. You think this is nerdy? You haven't heard the rest yet! Later in the holiday I found people in the hotel who were playing Scrabble – two guys my age who also seemed to be the stragglers-on at their school. I joined them and spent the rest of my nights getting my ass whooped whilst also feeling totally relaxed and at ease. I was drinking cheap Greek beer with two other people who were shy and quiet like me. Maybe this wasn't a party squad, perhaps we were missing out, but we were also doing what we wanted to, no pressure.

I've learnt it's quality over quantity when it comes to friendships. In a group setting I find myself trying extra hard to fit in (unless I find Scrabble aficionados). One-on-one, I know the friend likes me enough to hang out with me. I don't have to be someone else, someone different. One-on-one I know I can take up my friend's time and attention, which means it's easier to talk openly about anything I might be dealing with.

Most of my friends know about the difficult experiences I've had with my mental health. I usually test my tales of woe out with my bad comedy. I'll crack jokes about being a bit crazy or being on meds and if I feel that's met without any judgement (of course they are free to judge me on how shit my jokes are) then I might get serious.

Now, in my late twenties it's still hard for me to be 100 per cent honest with my friends, even the really good ones. It's the classic worry that I'll be a bummer or, even worse, a burden. I worry I can't be a good friend to them if I'm making everything about me and what I need. In my desire to never disclose my own issues I've missed out on genuine closeness with friends. It's too much of a one-way street to want to know everything about someone and only offer brief snippets of myself. I try to make a conscious effort to be a generous friend, a trusting friend and a little bit brave. I've told a few friends about my diagnoses and about self-harm. I've even learnt to ask some of them for help when shit hits the fan.

Telling someone about your mental health is daunting but important. It can mean that you dispel some of that heavy fog inside you. You're letting someone in, even if it's just a tiny bit, and it stops you from becoming isolated. Putting up a front and convincing people that I'm actually 100 per cent OK requires a lot of smokescreens. I have to overdo any good news I conjure up for myself just to make it sound believable: 'Oh yes, met up with that girl from work, it was great, so, so great! Had a really great, great time! Everything's great!' Even just looking at my Instagram during one of my lowest periods a year ago I can see a lot of photos of me at parties in pubs, looking like I'm having a great time, but with key giveaways: a bandage wrapped around my arm from elbow to wrist and eyes that are carrying the weight of three week's worth of crying.

Why telling your friends about how you're feeling is a good idea:

- ● You are not a burden. At their core people are good and they want to help each other, they just don't always know how to. Think about how

you feel when someone comes to you asking for
advice. I genuinely feel useful and even a slightly
bit honoured and I need to get it into my head
that it's the same the other way round

- You don't have to do everything by yourself.
  Battling a mental health problem, whether it's
  temporary or more permanent, is something that
  requires help. You need backup. Don't make this
  more difficult for yourself

- You're not crazy. Telling someone that your
  brain sometimes makes you feel like you're seeing
  things that aren't there, you're living in a dark
  well or there are ants crawling up and down your
  spine doesn't mean your friend will brand you as
  a loon and ditch you for good. Remember you're
  not crazy or weak or weird. Your symptoms, in
  whatever way they manifest, are happening to
  you, you didn't do anything to bring them on

Friendship can scoop you out of a low mood but friendship
isn't about being each other's personal saviours. You can't
magically fix someone's brain and you can't always fix
the shitty situation they're in. Friendship is about being
there, about showing up, about listening and about the
little things. Just having a friend send me photos of cute
dogs or a cucumber that looks remarkably like a large
penis means a lot. Just having someone fill my inbox

with things that make me laugh, no matter how childish, feels like they're there for me. They're not giving up.

My friends aren't trained therapists. I don't expect them to give me professional advice. Sometimes I'll explain how I'm feeling and they'll throw their hands up and say they genuinely have no idea what that feels like. I don't mind when they say that, it's not like they're shutting me down, they're just gently letting me know that I can't expect them to have a magic solution. A lot of this is new to them, and it's still quite new to me too.

Talking openly with your friends creates a dialogue that can often be surprising. When I told my best friend about my depression and how it was affecting my relationship at the time it was like something clicked for her. She felt like she'd been going through the exact same thing and couldn't figure out what it was exactly. She'd spent the last few weeks in bed wondering what the point of everything was. She'd requested a meeting with her tutor to drop out of her course and she hadn't spoken to anyone in days. She hadn't reached out to anyone because she felt lost and ashamed. She'd chosen isolation to give herself space and time to figure out what was wrong but got so used to her self-imposed solitude she couldn't get out of it. The escape route was blocked. She thought no one could help.

If I hadn't opened up about my own experience she might not have had her 'a ha' moment. For her, knowing that she wasn't the only one who felt that way came as a giant relief. She wasn't dying, her body wasn't slowly decaying. She had depression and she needed to talk to someone about it.

We still discuss our brain blips when we're together. Sometimes I get so excited about the fact she's describing something that feels exactly like what I'm going through I do a little squeal. She gets me! What a wonderful woman! I sometimes send her a text that starts with: 'Hey, do you ever feel . . . ?' or 'Do you think it's normal that . . . ?' Having someone I can send a quick burst of a worry to is invaluable. She doesn't have to respond straight away, just knowing that she'll read my query without judgement means everything.

Here are some things I wish people knew about my depression:

- I appreciate everything my friends and loved ones do for me and I'm sorry I'm not always able to show it
- I appreciate you making the effort to come to my house, but don't show up unannounced because it makes me feel tense and ashamed of how I've neglected myself and my surroundings. I need a warning
- If I seem distracted it's because half my head is filled with white noise

Maggy van Eijk

- If possible, hang out with me one-on-one because groups or new people freak me out
- I can watch a movie or TV show with you but nothing too long or in-depth because my concentration probably isn't great
- Make plans with me – not big, life-changing ones but little things like walks and picnics and going to the seaside. When I'm depressed, the future is a vast plane of nothingness; the more I can fill in the oppressive blanks the more I'll be able to cling onto hope
- When you say nice things to me I'm probably rolling my eyes or dismissing them but I am genuinely grateful
- Talking might be hard, sometimes it feels like there's a big blob of peanut butter in my mouth, so don't be scared if I don't say much or my words sound a bit garbled

Friends are also able to give you a bit of perspective. My doomsday thinking often requires someone outside of my own head to give me an injection of realism. The way I tend to think and treat myself in my lowest mood is quite horrible but I'm used to it, for me it's normal. I need a friend to make it clear to me that it's important I'm safe and well and I deserve better than self-destruction.

Telling your friend about what's going on with you doesn't have to be a big dramatic confession, it can be simply them asking how you are and you saying, 'Not so great, here's why . . .' But if you feel stressed about talking to them it might help to at least have the first sentence written down: 'I want to tell you about what's been going on for me', for example. That way you won't stumble in the beginning. You might also want to speak to someone anonymously first, like the Samaritans or SANE who both have phone and email services. You can test the water; decide what you'd like to share with your friend and what you're not quite comfortable with yet.

Personally, I've found it's useful to not blurt everything out in one go, and to choose people carefully – you don't have to tell everyone. I sometimes have a tendency to overshare where the words just spill out of me like water from a burst pipe and I immediately regret my outpouring. I end up berating myself for burdening that person with my problems. On some occasions my shame has gone so far I'll even put a stop to our friendship, genuinely believing I'm doing them a massive favour.

Go into the conversation with a good idea of what you want out of it. Is there something specific you could ask them to help with? No worries if there isn't, sometimes just sharing a situation with someone can make you feel lighter. If there is a more concrete thing your friend can help with definitely mention that, they'll be eager to help out.

It could be something small, like asking them to ring you so you get out of bed in time for an appointment. Or perhaps you just want them to sit and watch a movie with you once a week. Can they help you start a difficult conversation with your parents? Can they meet you after a therapy session so you have someone to talk to? If it's a big ask, keep in mind that they might say no. Don't see this as rejection. Maybe they had too much on their plate? Maybe they felt like they weren't the right person to help you?

As a caveat to all of this about how amazing friendship can be, there are times in our lives where it might feel that you simply don't have anyone close enough to you that you can talk to. That's OK. There's nothing wrong or broken about you.

If someone decides to tell you about their mental health issues and you're feeling a bit Oh-God-How-Will-I-Deal-With-This about it, here are some things to bear in mind:

- Your end goal can't be to fix them. Even if you're unable to cheer them up, that isn't failing. Your goal is to simply listen
- Just because you might see them smiling

doesn't mean they're all of a sudden doing fine.
Remember: people are excellent performers and
we select what we want to show the outside world

- If someone doesn't respond to your messages or is
  a bit blunt when you ask if they're OK don't jump
  to the conclusion that they're mad at you. Often
  it's because they don't feel like they deserve your
  kind words so they block them out. Don't give up

- If something is making you feel uncomfortable or
  you're worried, tell a third party, don't freak out
  and disappear

- Remember that your friend is trying their best,
  even if it looks like they've put in minimal effort.
  They're really, really trying

- Let them know you care but don't pity them.
  Don't treat them like they're broken

- Don't make them feel like their problems aren't
  valid: e.g. 'A lot of people have it worse than you'
  or 'People are dying in Africa' or 'Well, maybe
  I should be the one cutting myself!' Your friend
  could be incredibly sensitive. Whilst you're only
  human, try not to unleash any frustration. Don't
  snap and say things like: 'Just get over it!' or 'Just
  get out of bed for god's sake' – this won't work.
  Tough love might work for personal trainers but
  that's not a good foundation for friendship. A
  partner once said to me, 'YOU'RE feeling suicidal?

Your suicidalness is making ME feel suicidal!', which did not go down well for us

- Make them feel like you are a team and that you're in it together, even if they're the ones battling the demons

- A simple spontaneous text can make someone's day

- Remember it's OK to be scared. If your friend is severely depressed and their world view is incredibly bleak, some of the things they might share with you can be shocking. You might even find yourself getting caught up in their way of thinking and suddenly the world doesn't seem as bright as it did before. Make sure you have someone else you can talk to as well to offload when you need to

- Get professional intervention. If your friend is talking about suicide and plans to kill themselves it's not on you to stop them. You have to tell a relative or your local mental health facility because their life could be in danger. You're not a trained psychologist, this isn't on you

THERAPY

I've been in therapy, on and off, since I was sixteen. In total, I've seen seven different therapists – my favourite being the one I have at the time of writing this. She's very no-nonsense and doesn't let me get away with glossing over things that are really affecting me. I've had times where I've walked out of her offices thinking, 'She's a bitch I hate her' and then I cool down and remember she's doing her job. She's able to rip the Band-Aid off even when the Band-Aid is clinging on for dear life.

My current therapy focuses on connecting current issues with larger themes in my life. There's a lot of introspection and talking about the past. I've had other types of therapy that were more practical, where we set goals and I had to carry out specific tasks in between sessions. These tasks would be things like giving my mood a score or pinpointing where in the day anxiety struck the most: what was I doing, what happened? These sessions used something called CBT, cognitive behavioural therapy, which is what GPs often recommend when you seek help for anxiety and depression.

Later on, I began seeing therapists who specialised in interpersonal therapy where they go a little bit more into your childhood, relationship history and your past in general. You get a lot of 'a ha' moments where suddenly a big chunk of what makes you you clicks into place. There are big things in your life that have a significant impact on you that sometimes only someone with a bit of distance and a fresh perspective can point out (oh and years of training).

There are lots of different types of therapy available and before you settle on a therapist I recommend you do as much research as possible and try to figure out what will work for you. I ended up going from one to the other without putting much thought into why I chose a therapist. Often it was because I was using a free service – if you're finally at the top of a waiting list you don't want to be picky.

Don't do what I did. Instead of agreeing to whatever is made available to you, ask about the type of therapy being offered and Google it. CBT helped me set the foundation for getting my life back when anxiety was hell-bent on destroying it. It gave me tools and tricks to keep panic attacks under control – tools I still use to this day. Thanks to CBT methods I was able to get out of my house, on a bus and even to a party.

When I felt like I had the tools under my belt, I was eager to learn why my body reacts to certain situation in such a dramatic way. The more free-talking forms of therapy helped me do that. There are fewer take-home tips but eventually I learnt how to be more sympathetic to myself. My body isn't broken, my brain isn't sabotaging me; there are reasons why I react the way I do.

Often the first session with your therapist will be a trial: you test out if the two of you get along and if it's likely the therapist will actually be able to help you. I never really paid too much attention to this part. It felt like I was having to just regurgitate my life story, which I'd done many times before. If the therapist was nice and able to laugh at my dark humour I thought we were pretty much sorted. I didn't pay attention to the details. Did I feel listened to? Did I feel comfortable? Were either of us more focused on the clock than what was going on in the room?

Whilst I have had some great therapists and counsellors, not all of them have been right for me. My favourite being a large man called Nigel with papery white skin that showed off every red blotch across his cheeks. I felt like he couldn't relate to my stories. I felt myself changing my language, trying to avoid any judgement I suspected he was passing on me. It didn't help by the fact that instead of saying, 'Are you promiscuous?' or 'What is your attitude towards sex?' he'd say things like 'So how do you feel about sexy times?'

I've also had a therapist who I liked too much. I wanted to be her friend outside of the tiny room we met in every Wednesday evening. When I was planning my solo trip to Paris I had to stop myself from inviting her along. She was warm and kind and gave me good advice. I transferred onto her the idea of what I thought a woman should be. She was put together, well-adjusted but also sympathetic and caring.

I wanted to please her so badly that whenever she'd make an observation about my life I'd eagerly nod and agree without actually thinking, 'Wait, is this right?' I wanted so much to be a good client and I wanted her to feel like she was doing a good job. My instinct has always been to blend in with my surrounds, adapt and be whatever the situation demands of me. It's how you survive but this isn't ideal for therapy. My job isn't to protect the therapist's feelings or to make them feel good about their career choice.

So how do you know if you HAVE found a good therapist?

Most importantly, you feel like you can share what you're feeling without fear of shame. This probably won't happen straight away. In the beginning I find myself talking about 'easy' things: a stressful meeting I had, a difficult conversation or a break-up that happened ages ago. These are easy for me because they're not at the top of my list of things that keep me awake at night. Once we get into a rhythm in our sessions I peel my protective layers away and start divulging things that affect me more.

Shame is such a big part of my life. It engulfs me, pulls me away from healthy choices. It stuffs my throat with cotton wool and yaps at my ankles like a stray animal. When shame infiltrates therapy it stops you from getting to the heart of what's troubling you. I found a way around this when I started voicing the shame out loud, almost like breaking the 'fourth wall' of therapy.

A session with my current therapist started as normal with a 'How has your week been?' and, to be frank, my week had been a disaster. I'd had too much to drink, fought with my boyfriend at the time, who I was pretty sure had a drug problem, and ended up in a hotel room in Shoreditch with an ex who I was having a toxic sexual text exchange with. I felt so ashamed about my actions and my lack of self-control. I didn't have a handle on anything it seemed. I needed to vent but I was scared my therapist would think I was a drunk, a whore and, at best, morally bankrupt.

Instead of getting into what I wanted to say I talked about a presentation I had to do at work where I felt like I hadn't performed well but that it was OK because I'd also not smoked for three days and I was getting stuck in a good book so I had something to be proud of.

My therapist must have felt that in between these two anecdotes was the weight of something else. She asked me to stop and explain what was going on in my head in that very moment. That to me felt easy. I just had to say what was going on in my mind.

'I feel a bit useless.'

'Why is that?'

And here's where it got trickier.

'I want to tell you something that happened but I'm worried you'll think I'm an awful person, even though I know it's your job to listen without judgement, and I'm not saying you're bad at your job, I'm just worried.'

Then she said what has now become her catchphrase: 'OK, there's a lot going on there.'

We unpacked my sentence word by word and examined the feelings behind them. I realised that I was passing the shame I was feeling about myself on to her. Coming to this conclusion helped me untangle what I wanted to say from the webby strands of shame and I got it all out there.

Sometimes in therapy it can feel like it's a very routine exchange: your therapist asks you a question and you answer, but actually the hardest things to say don't come out that easily. Breaking the wall of therapy really helped me in that situation. It drove me away from that question–answer–question–answer structure. I was able to stop and share what I was feeling in the moment. Since then I've always paused the session when I feel the need to acknowledge when I feel awkward or fearful.

My therapist also asks me a lot about how I'm feeling physically, which helps me connect my mind and body. Often, if I'm talking about something stressful I feel spaced out and floaty so I need something to bring me back down to earth again.

Another thing I have learnt not to do in therapy is treat it like a trial for a new stand-up routine. I consider myself to have a big Mary Poppins-style never-ending bag of flaws but if I had to point to one thing about myself I like it's that I know how to make people laugh. When friends are down I can comfort them and say something that'll make them smile, even just for a little bit. The problem for fans of humour, though, is that you use that humour in your storytelling all the time, even when it's perhaps not totally appropriate. In therapy, whenever I'm talking about self-harm or suicide or sexual assault, I inject a dark joke in there somewhere. It's more for my own protection than anyone else's. I don't want it to get too serious, I don't want to think too much and I don't want to feel sorry for myself. Ever.

This meant that when a therapist laughed at one of my jokes or anecdotes I considered this to be a big win. I once made a counsellor laugh three times in a row and I walked out of there feeling like I'd just secured a spot on *SNL*. Turning my pain into laughter felt like a win. I was doing something productive. My therapist now (can you tell I'm mildly obsessed with her?) has steered me away from using her as an audience member to *The Maggy Show*.

I was filling her in on the past year, how I had to have a disciplinary hearing at work because I'd lied to hide my mental health condition. How I was drinking too much. How an ambulance had to take me to a mental health unit but also how even that was kind of funny because the ambulance dude was my age and he kept trying to make awkward small talk. I was going through the highs and lows of my life like I'd just chugged three cans of Red Bull. I wasn't taking much of a breath and after a quick inhale that sounded more like a shriek she stopped me. 'Can you just pause there?' I did but I was taken aback, 'Why was she interrupting my story?' She told me I was breezing through these details of my life that were important, but I was breezing through them like a shopping list and my slightly manic 'THIS IS ALL OK DON'T WORRY' tone was actually making her feel anxious.

'I'm making YOU feel anxious?' I thought. 'What? I'm not doing anything. I'm just sitting here telling my story like I'm supposed to.' Afterwards I realised that the way I was talking about my life mirrored the way I felt about my life. It was all a joke. I felt disconnected from it and deep down I was scared I wasn't going to make it out alive.

My therapist taught me to take my sessions more seriously. Before I start telling her something I try to connect with how I really feel about it. It doesn't mean I then have to go ahead and talk in a sad, meek little voice. I still breeze through a lot of things, but I try to slow down. I find it hard to access my 'real' feelings, the ones that are buried deep down somewhere, and I'm still not there if I'm honest. But the more I slow down and try and notice what's going on, the closer I feel like I'm getting to achieving that.

This isn't the case for everyone, but for me I think it's important that my therapist is a woman. With Nigel, who was never able to say 'sex', I didn't feel like I could tell him about my relationship problems, my promiscuity or intrusive sexual thoughts. I've been known to throw in a couple of 'ban men' rants whenever I get too angry at something a man has done to me and it's not ideal if the person sitting opposite me has a penis. I would be too scared of offending him.

I've also deliberately not gone for a therapist once because she used a very glamorous 1980s-style headshot on her LinkedIn profile, which seemed weird. I'm always mildly intimidated by my therapists, as I am by any woman who seems smart and put together, and I don't want to feel like I have to come in dressed to impress. I go to therapy after a busy day at work or a busy day of being depressed in bed so I'm going to look dishevelled at best.

I've also gotten on with therapists the best who are foreign in the country they're practicing in. As someone who's been living in the UK for five years since I chose to study here I get on the most with people who can empathise with feeling a bit alien and out of place. When Brexit happened I had a therapist who, like me, faced an uncertain future and she was able to put some of my worries in context.

These are all little details I've found help me when choosing my therapist. It's different for everyone but when you find someone you connect with it can feel like a massive relief. Of course that process isn't exactly easy.

Maggy van Eijk

THE WAITING GAME

The one thing I wish someone had told me about therapy is that once you decide it's something you think might be good for you, you won't get it straight away. Unless you go private, which doesn't *have* to be super expensive but will cost money, you'll more than likely end up on some waiting list of sorts.

Every country is different, but living in the UK it's hard to avoid how incredibly underfunded the NHS is. There simply aren't enough mental health facilities to meet everyone's needs. I've spoken to hundreds of people who have been ignored by the system or ended up with the wrong treatment because there wasn't anything else available to them.

I'm currently experiencing the joy of trying to get dialectical behavioural therapy for my difficulties with borderline personality disorder. I've been on the phone with my mental health services on and off for three months now, trying to find the appropriate group in my borough. During the last conversation I was told they had no space anywhere and I was sent a list of self-help websites, which feels exactly like ending up back at square one.

This story isn't a unique one, and there are many people who are worse off. I'm lucky I'm not at risk at the moment. I'm not in danger, I'm unlikely to cause myself or others any deliberate harm, but if I was, it's terrifying to know there'd be a massive gap before I could see anyone.

In my quest to get my mental health back on track, I realised that there are A LOT of phone calls involved. I hate speaking on the phone. I still have to take a deep breath before picking up even if it's my boyfriend calling. So having to sort my life out by calling a dozen people, telling them all my problems and sometimes practically begging for help isn't something I consider very fun.

So what do you do when you're in between appointments and it feels like you have to wait a lifetime before you get any help?

- Ask your GP for a list of all the crisis numbers in your area you can call in an emergency situation when you're worried about what you might do to yourself. Put these in a folder and keep them somewhere safe. Some of them will be phone numbers you can call (e.g. your nearest A&E department) but others might be places you can walk in. My borough in London has what they call 'Crisis Cafe' where you can go in to receive peer support in times of serious distress
- Keep a diary of any appointments or phone assessments so you can chase services up if they're going over the time within which they said they'd ring you back
- Look for support groups in your area you can

turn to if you feel comfortable in that kind of peer-to-peer setting

- Keep a journal of thoughts, feelings and moods to track how you're doing. That way, when you are finally at the top of a list and you get seen you can easily outline what's been going on for you in the recent months

- Try out any mental health apps and websites you might find useful. I don't respond that well to apps, especially meditation ones, but whilst I was waiting for a therapist I'd take an hour every Tuesday evening for a meditation session in the comfort of my living room. It gave me a sense of routine and structure. I felt like I was still doing something, despite being in a bit of a limbo

- Similarly buy a book (buy my book – again!) and immerse yourself in writing that seems useful to you. Keep trying until you find something that sticks

- Try to single out a block of time every day where all you do is relax. You're not working or online or stressing about anything. You're doing whatever it is that helps you zone out and breathe deeply: putting on a face mask, wrapping yourself up in a duvet accompanied by a Harry Potter book or chilling in the bath. Stick to this time. It's important

MEDICATION

When I was first prescribed antidepressants, it happened very quickly. I spoke to my doctor about what was going on, she asked me a series of five questions, which I answered, and without so much as a blink she prescribed me Citalopram.

I went home feeling extremely confused. This felt like a big deal. It felt like a massive life change I was embarking on, but it happened within the space of a few minutes. I collected my prescription from the pharmacy and put the pills down on my living room table. I talked it over with my uni boyfriend P. and we decided I should take them; they were a low dosage anyway, and if they weren't right for me I'd stop taking them. I swallowed my first pill and sat on our hand-me-down sofa waiting for something to happen.

A year later I went off them. My anxiety was nowhere near as bad – I was able to get on trains, I'd gotten a job and moved to London – and I was doing OK. Getting off them wasn't easy. My brain felt like streetview on Google Maps when you click the arrow and the view moves in this slow, glitchy way. I'd be doing my job or getting ready for bed and a brain glitch occurred. It was scary but it didn't last long; in a week or two I was back to leading my glitchless life.

About three years later my anxiety returned, together with deep depression and suicidal thoughts that hovered over me like a persistent cloud. I was given a new prescription, this time higher. Because Citalopram had worked so well for me before it seemed like a good avenue to go down.

A couple of months later and things hadn't really improved; my self-harm was out of hand and I kept getting flashing images of hurling my body in front of a car. They upped my prescription. A couple of months later I came back, complained again about the self-harm and they upped my dosage again.

I know from the outside this sounds like the doctors were just trying to silence me with pills and to be honest it did feel like that. When you're desperate for a solution you'll take whatever your doctor will give you. But what I do know is that medication does genuinely help me. It makes me think more clearly so I have the headspace to counteract some of my intrusive thoughts. It also makes my anxiety symptoms more manageable.

Before you agree to take anything, look into what pills are being prescribed to you. This does unfortunately mean you have to navigate a gazillion scare stories about all the awful things that have happened to people on them. Do your research carefully, stick to outlets you trust and don't let yourself get freaked out by other people's horror stories. Read medical sites and speak to helplines.

When your GP is thinking about giving you medication ask as many questions as possible so you don't go home and spend the whole night worrying. Ask what happens to your mood, your sex life, your physical health and what will happen when you decide to stop taking them. Make sure you have follow-up appointments so you can check in with how you're doing. If possible, try and see the same GP in this period so you build up a rapport and you get used to talking to them about your mental health.

Also, remember that there is no wonder pill that will cure your symptoms. When I received a diagnosis that was new to me – borderline personality disorder – I thought, well, at least I get to go on different meds now and maybe this new one will make me happy instantly! My psychiatrist told me that if I did want to change to stronger meds I'd probably have trouble concentrating during the day. I shrugged and said I could deal with that but enquired what it would do for my reading. I was reading a book a day at that time, reading was everything.

'Oh, reading might be hard, your brain might not be able to focus on all the words.'

'Well screw that,' I thought at that point. 'I'll stick to what I'm doing.' Reading is my natural antidepressant, I don't want to be without it.

There is also no one-size-fits-all pill. There are different types that work for different people and sometimes it takes a bit of trial and error to find the one that is right for you. There's a period that usually lasts a few weeks where your body is adjusting and things get a bit wobblier at this time. Don't panic, this is normal.

You also have to remember that you don't have to be on antidepressants your whole life. It's a bit like getting a cast when you break a leg. The cast is there to help you heal and to support your damaged leg. With the right lifestyle changes, physical therapy and a good support network the leg will heal to a healthy point and you can take that cast off.

Here are some things medication definitely isn't:

- It's not something you can only resort to when things get REALLY REALLY BAD. People who opt for meds aren't necessarily at breaking point, they just need some extra support
- Meds aren't fake happiness. My meds don't give me a dose of fabricated emotions. I'm depressed but I'm not a robot. Meds pave a little way through the darkness to allow me to feel happiness, but they're not the happiness itself
- They don't change the fundamental things that make you who you are. They won't alter your

personality. For me, meds help me realise who I
am and who I could be if I work hard, get help
and be kind to myself

- Taking meds doesn't make you weak. It makes
  you proactive. You're taking charge of your
  situation
- Meds won't kill your creativity. Depression makes
  me unable to think imaginatively or even want to.
  Depression makes it so that I can't get out of bed
  or switch my laptop on to write something
- Your meds won't turn you into a raging drug
  addict
- Once you go off your meds you won't turn into
  a hysterical banshee. However, you might find
  that you'll end up crying a lot. Your brain has
  been flattening out a lot of your emotions whilst
  you were medicated so it needs a period of
  adjustment to figure out what kinds of responses
  are normal. If you're a *Grey's Anatomy* fan you'll
  remember Cristina Yang's heart-breaking crying
  scene after the loss of her baby. She yells: 'I can't
  stop!' in between fits of tears and hyperventilation
  and no one knows what to do until she screams:
  'SOMEONE SEDATE ME!' This is how I've felt in
  the period I came off my meds. Not because I lost
  a child but for less traumatic things like not being
  able to find my keys, my train being delayed or

curdled milk I was counting on for my cereal.
Whilst this might sound insufferable it never lasts
long. Like Cristina Yang I rode it out and in a few
weeks I was back to kicking ass

REMEMBER THiS
WhEN THiNGS ARe
GETTiNG BETTEr

It had been a year since the episode when I burnt my arm
outside of the pub. Things were better but I still felt
the same. I felt like that sad lost person. My wounds had
healed, I didn't have to wear a sleeve of bandages any
more, but I felt listless and tired of being tired.

A group of friends was having a birthday party that I
wanted to go to. My dating life was in a bit of a shambles
and I wanted to be around people who could make me
laugh (and potentially post a pic of me laughing so the
guy I was dating would see all the great fun I was having
without him). The group of friends decided they wanted
to go to the exact same pub I'd been to that fateful
evening, a year before. Apparently there aren't enough

pubs in Stoke Newington that London media people like to go to.

An itching optimism within me made me feel like it would be all right to go. At the very least, it was a better option than staying home pining over some guy I didn't think liked me. No one there would know what had happened the last time I'd been to that pub, but for safety I went with my friend who *had* been there. He knew this place would be a bit of a minefield for me so he became my fire exit. If I needed a quick escape I could use him.

Getting ready for this party felt like preparing for battle. There were things I needed to have in place. I told myself I couldn't smoke or drink too much (after two glasses of wine I was going to switch to Diet Coke). I also felt like I needed to arm myself with things that *were* going to be productive. I stuck on a YouTube tutorial and caked myself in make-up. Foundation and concealer were my camouflage. They made me feel powerful, like I was ready for anything. I wore a dress I loved, some fancy shoes and I went to my friend's beforehand so we could go in together. I had a water bottle and some gum in my bag, and a book in case I needed to go off and read. You never know.

I felt a shiver when I walked in, past the flicker of fairy lights. The pub was full of people and the odd dog here and there. My friends had a swarm of other friends around them so if I needed to bail it could go relatively unnoticed. There was nothing tying me to the pub; I wasn't trapped, I was in there by my own volition. I could leave when I wanted to: I was in control.

I took a seat on the fringes of the group and tried to settle into the conversation. Most of these friends were from work so it was easy to go into office politics and the new office fridge and how terrible the sofa in reception was. Whilst everyone chipped in I glanced behind me. There was the table I'd been sitting at a year ago. Tonight it was occupied by a couple sharing a bottle of red wine. They looked so calm, like they'd decided to go for a drink before returning home to a night of watching episodes of a show they loved. Their peacefulness seemed so unlike anything I had felt when I had been sitting there myself.

Someone asked me what I'd been doing with my weekend so far and I reeled myself back into the conversation. I said something about watching a true crime documentary and returned the question. It was a bit like playing that hot potato game in school, when you stand in a circle and everyone tosses a little beanbag around until the music stops. Whoever has the 'hot potato' in their hand has to leave the game. For me, having to lead the conversation was that hot potato. This night was stressful enough, I just wanted to lean back and listen to everyone else talk. I also needed enough space to tackle those intrusive thoughts should they arise.

Sitting, listening and sipping my wine slowly helped me last two hours without any freak-outs. My only issue was that I was tired and I could feel my eyelids drooping a little. The friend who'd come to the party with me suggested we go back home and I felt like I was ready. We watched the true crime documentary I'd not actually seen on his projection. We toasted with a big bag of crisps, some hummus and a cans of Coke. I'd made it. I'd proved to myself I could handle a stressful situation. I rode it out. I was kind to myself and I caught up with my friends. I did it.

A few days later I tried to think back to what had made that event such a win for me. Stripping myself of any sharp objects and cigarettes and lighters was a smart move. I didn't feel like I was policing myself or being my own strict parent. I was actually allowing myself to have a good time, to stay present in the moment. When I needed the bathroom I peed and went back out again. I didn't sit and scratch lines into my hands. I didn't pinch my thigh until it bruised. I wanted to get back, to participate and to listen. Giving myself that risk-free night was actually a very kind and thoughtful present to myself.

I haven't been back to that pub since. Unless I absolutely have to I don't think I'll go back anytime soon. Whilst I had a good evening, it's very much time for new pubs, for new routines and new memories.

For me, the notion of 'recovery' is having several experiences like the one I just described. But it's not always going to be foolproof. Recovery isn't a before and after photo. It's not a straightforward journey from one point to another. There are times when I get pulled back in. Where I seem to shake off everything I've learnt. There are times, even now, when I return to self-harming, I drink too much, I act irrationally or dangerously, I push someone away. Usually in the aftermath of these times I make it worse by scolding myself for not having learnt anything. I hurt myself and look in the mirror and think: 'Come on, surely I'm too old for this shit? Don't I know better?'

Just because you have all the tools doesn't mean you'll always know exactly how to use them. However, with each setback the time it takes for me to regain control, to find the right tool, decreases. Instead of full months spiralling out of control I can limit it to weeks. Sometimes I can recognise the symptoms and get ready. Prepare for battle.

It's so easy for me to beat myself up. It's easy for me to talk down on myself. It's much harder to be kind. To stop and be proud of what I've done so far. To be proud that I've asked for help, that I've gone to appointments, that I've shared my problems instead of letting them fester inside me. There may be days when it all comes flooding back, but that's OK. This isn't a makeover in an American TV show. I'm not going to walk out on stage wheeling a cart filled with meat illustrating all the fat I've lost. This isn't a brand spanking new version of myself. This is the same me, just slightly braver, and slightly better prepared, and I still might have to leave the stage for a bit to go deal with some stuff but BRB – I'll be back again, don't worry.

I'm also coming to understand that my brain isn't my enemy; there are times when anxiety, for example, has actively protected me. When my uncle passed away after a brave and devastating battle with cancer, I returned to the Netherlands for his funeral. With my dad and siblings beside me, we were part of the procession walking into the church. It was incredibly hard seeing the pain amongst my uncle's immediate family – my cousins and aunty and my dad, his brother.

I turned away from my dad who was blinking away tears. I looked around me and noticed how many people were there. There must have been hundreds. My brain decided to tell me it would be really, really awful if I tripped over right now. Can you imagine? What if you tripped someone else up too and they tripped someone and BOOM the coffin would fall. It would all be your fault!

When I made it to my seat unscathed I still couldn't relax. All the usual fears came up: imagine if you vomit right now, imagine if you pass out, everyone will think you're such a drama queen, everyone will think you're trying to steal the limelight at a fucking funeral.

I knew I couldn't give into my fears. I had to be there. I couldn't run off. My siblings were on one side of me and my dad on the other. I tried to remember what I'd learnt. I got out my mental toolkit. OK. Breathe. Breathe properly. I filled my lungs with air and let it out, slowly, through my mouth. I relaxed my shoulders, clenched and unclenched my fists and told myself to ride it out. And I did.

After the funeral it took a few days for me to shake the nervous tension I'd carried since the church. When I flew back to London it slowly faded like snow at the end of winter. Day by day it disappeared a little until it seemed to be gone completely. It was then that it suddenly hit me. The fog cleared and there was one resounding message for my brain to tackle: my uncle is dead. My dad didn't have a brother any more. My aunty had lost her husband and my cousins their dad. Not to mention the hundreds of people in the church, they'd all lost someone too.

I can't grieve around other people. I sneak off to quiet corners and cry by myself. That day at the church, my anxiety had given me something to focus on, to put all my attention in until I was ready to let go and to feel the weight of my uncle's passing. I was weirdly grateful for my strange brain. For once it was trying to do me a favour.

RECOVERY

Recovery is about learning, about moving forward one step at a time. When I have a setback, I find myself completely absorbed in negativity, it rolls around my head like laundry in the washing machine. Everything is shrouded in a dark haze. I find it hard to just feel 'a little bit bad', it's always a near-catastrophic END OF THE WORLD feeling for me.

As I'm trying to get better, I've found it incredibly important to cling onto the little things that make me happy. Small steps I can make to offer myself a rope and dig my mind out of its blackhole. Here are some of those things I've found I can lean on to make the catastrophe feel a little less catastrophic:

LISTS

You've made it this far in the book, so you've probably gathered I appreciate a good list. I can't say enough good things about them. Lists impose a sense of organisation; without lists I feel totally adrift.

My room is a burial site for completed and half-completed lists. There's not a day that goes by without some kind of list-making. Even on holiday I make a list of the books I want to read, or how long I want to suntan for before I get a heat rash. Lists break down the stickier problems in life. 'Make more money' becomes slightly more attainable when you read it as 'pitch freelance articles to so-and-so', 'make all your lunches for the week on a Sunday', 'chase old housemate for the money they owe'.

I can divide my lists into the future and the past. Goals and to-do lists are about the future, even if it's as immediate as what I'm going to be doing in the next half an hour. Some lists act as a little step-ladder into the past. I'll make a list of all the things I think have been bothering me that day. What am I hung up on? What's making me feel uncomfortable? What does this feeling remind me of?

It's funny that my first big career job at BuzzFeed involved making lists. As a staff writer I'd take some kind of identity fixture: 'being shy' or 'being a bookworm' or 'being the eldest sibling' and break those things down into a variety of headings. Plenty of people look down on this style of writing but doing this for almost three years taught me that lists tell a story. OK, not a big exploration into the human psyche type story, but the BuzzFeed-style list has a narrative, a start and a finish.

This is how I approach lists outside of BuzzFeed too. I imagine myself at the end, once I've completed the tasks and deadlines. How will I feel at the end? How can I achieve that feeling?

When I used to own *The Sims* (I'm yet to find a laptop fast enough to continue playing my beloved game), I had a very particular way of playing. I'd take a character (usually remarkably similar to myself or someone I wanted to sleep with). Press pause. Fill up the top screen with actions I wanted them to undertake. Then I'd hit play and just sit there and watch the actions unfold – hopefully getting that red bar back to green or finally getting that couple to make a baby. It stressed me out clicking the actions whilst the game was in play mode. I needed that time to pause, to think. I also wanted to revel in that almost euphoric relief I felt just after I'd planned a set of actions. I've done the hard bit now, the worst is over. Let's see the results.

I am my own Sim. Sometimes this approach feels a bit robotic but it gives me that sense of control. Even on a day where I have absolutely nothing to do, a lazy Sunday morning, where your only task is relieving your bladder whenever you can be bothered to get out of bed, even on days like that I'll make a list. It might say: 'Finish reading that chapter, read that gossip blog, send your friend a dog meme.' None of that is particularly hard to achieve but it makes me feel good that I have.

Lists also help me create a sense of continuity. For me, depression and dissociation blur the day into a cloud of nothingness. I've had days where I've had to stop what I'm doing just to lie down on the floor. It's not that I'm tired, it's just that there seems to be no possible way to continue on with what I'm doing. Instead I just lie there completely still. The only way to climb out of this state is to get thinking about a list of things to do. Just keep going. Do that one thing. Go from the beginning to the end. You can do it.

PHONE APPS

My phone casts a lot of 'bad vibes'. I can be in a perfectly good mood and decide to have a look at what that girl who may or may not be dating my ex is up to and suddenly my soul feels obliterated. After the break-up with R. the Casanova guy from the theatre I was left reeling more than usual and I found myself unable to stop thinking about him. It colonised every inch of my brain. I replayed the break-up over and over again. I went over everything I'd done to make him break up with me. I went over everything I said. He wanted space from me and we weren't speaking so my thoughts had nowhere to go but swarm around my skull.

I tried to get out of the house. I went to a play with an old friend and tried to see an exhibition by my favourite photographer, but nothing helped. Everything reminded me of him – every place, every image – until eventually I gave up, went home and completely gave into the break-up loop.

On the train home from an exhibition by William Burroughs (who was always my problematic literary crush) I felt defeated by another utterly useless afternoon of not being able to connect to something I was so passionate about. I watched the guy next to me play *Candy Crush*. I hadn't thought about that game in a while. I'd obsessively played for a month and given up thanks to all the extra features they make you pay for.

On the spot I downloaded it from my app store and started playing. The initial levels are quite easy to pass so you get an instant dose of satisfaction. From then on it's mostly luck. Correct me if you're a *Candy Crush* pro, but there's not a tremendous amount of skill involved.

Before I knew it my train had reached its station and I hadn't thought about my ex at all. In my flat I waved hi to my housemates and crawled into bed. I'd made a list of break-up movies I thought would help me through this time. I'd gotten through about five and next up was *Swingers* with Vince Vaughn. Vaughn looks absolutely nothing like my ex, but my eyes moulded his jaw and his slanted side smile into my ex's and before I knew it the film was ruined. I shut my laptop off and closed my eyes, unable to escape my own thoughts.

I grabbed my phone and began *Candy Crush* where I'd left off. I could feel my mind trying to pull away, to go back to the pit of my break-up misery but I wanted to get to the next level more than I wanted to wallow. I played it for hours upon hours. My focus hadn't been this sharp in days. It was night-time and I realised I hadn't cried since the exhibition. This was progress! A friend texted asking if I was OK and I replied, 'Hanging in there X', which was the most positive response I'd had for anyone in weeks. I went back to my game and played until 3am and then I slept. I dreamt of bulging candies bursting happily over my head.

I eventually kicked the *Crush* habit once my brain was able to not think about my ex on its own accord. I started reading again, watching movies properly and even writing slightly angsty poems – but it helped.

I'm definitely not suggesting you will drive your depression away by spending every second of the day on a game on your phone. For me, deleting the usual social media suspects that make me feel shit and instead spending my time bursting candy canes was a definite improvement. It gave me some structure to the day – I was able to get out of bed and on the train. It even gave me something to look forward to. I ended up getting to level 90. I don't know if that's good, please don't tell me if it's not.

DOGS

When I see a dog, a part of my brain emits a high-pitched squeal and all I can think about is getting as close to that dog as possible. Best case scenario is that I get to pet the dog, but if there are things in the way or the owner seems particularly wearied by a deranged blonde lady running up to their pet I can be content with just seeing the dog.

No dog is like another; they're so unique, contradictory

and clever. I like old dogs the most. Dogs that have lived a little, that give you the impression they can tell you stories from the Great Dog War of '09. I love dogs who want to protect you a little, who know when you're sad and rest their head on your lap.

One of the nicest things anyone has ever done for me involves a dog. It was after my sexual assault, recurring visits to A&E and a bout of depression that brought me so low I didn't know how I was going to claw myself out again.

My friend D. told me to come meet him in Crouch End, which was pretty far away from where I lived. I didn't want to leave the house let alone make a long journey through London. My brain was overly sensitive to stimuli. Just the idea of crossing the road made my head hurt. However, D. insisted and I knew, deep down, I needed to be around people. I'd been left alone to my own devices for too long and it wasn't looking pretty.

I got up, skipped brushing my teeth for the sixth morning in a row and put on a bleach-stained hoodie that used to belong to my mum. I hoped I didn't bump into anyone on my way there, but my hood was up and the stale smell of sweat from my pits would keep most people at bay. When I got to Finsbury Park I met D. and we took a bus further north to Crouch End. Whilst he talked, I put my head on his shoulder and pretended I was still in bed.

At Crouch End we sat and chatted on a park bench for a bit. I was getting increasingly annoyed – I mean, I could've sat on a park bench nearer to my house. When it hit 2pm, D. got a text and I made some joke that if he was going to text one of his many female admirers I was going to go home.

He ignored me and made me follow him across the street towards a house on the corner. I still had no idea what was going on, I was pretty sure he didn't know anyone in Crouch End, especially not someone who owned this beautiful mansion. An incredibly glamorous lady opened the door. She had golden hair that resembled the colour of my own, when I actually washed it. She said hi to D. and then handed us the most beautiful golden retriever I'd ever seen in my life. 'Thanks for walking Milo,' she said. 'Bring him back whenever you're done, no rush!'

She closed the door and I stared at D., not quite believing that my favourite ever animal in the whole world was currently sniffing my battered Converse shoes: 'Is this real?'

'Yep, let's go walk Milo.'

Turns out D., a keen user of dating apps, had finally found an app that is worth everyone's time: Borrow My Doggy. It's an app where dog owners and dog lovers can connect and help each other out. D. had walked Milo before and his owners were so pleased they let D. come along and take Milo whenever he wanted.

Milo was a wonderful creature. I made D. hold him on the leash so I could spend my time running ahead and staring at his wonderful face. When we walked around the park I was astounded that some people walked past without even noticing him. I felt like shouting, 'Come on people! Look at this beautiful dog. Look at him!'

At the park cafe, Milo sat patiently by us whilst we ate sandwiches. For me, the magic of Milo was that he demanded all of my attention – not because he was a hassle but because he was so beautiful and gentle and I couldn't stop staring at him. My whole focus was on seeing what he was doing, what his expression was, how he was walking, what he was smelling. He was a little escape path out of my depression, even if it was just for a day.

The rest of the afternoon was pure joy. It made me think about the future – perhaps I'd own a dog like Milo one day. Walking Milo helped me get out and stretch my legs and breathe in some air that hadn't been trapped in my room for weeks.

If someone you love is struggling (and they happen to be animal lovers) take them to the zoo or the aquarium on a quiet day in the week. Go walk a dog or go to a farm. Remind them that animals exist, and loving animals is such a simple yet restorative thing. Milo reminded me of all the dogs of my childhood, the ones who saw me cry, who caught my tennis balls. Milo also gave me a well-needed break from myself for a bit. Hope you're reading this Milo.

LAW & ORDER

A lot of TV shows are presented to us in one big drop, giving you the option to watch the entire thing from start to finish in one go without eating properly, or getting dressed. You can just sit there, becoming one with your couch, only occasionally reminding yourself you need to pee.

There's a comfort for me in bingeing when I'm depressed that I don't think is all bad. When my head is filled with static it's impossible to concentrate on anything. I can't read, I can't sleep and I can't listen to anyone. What I *can* do is follow a TV show that I've either seen many times before, something like *Seinfeld* or *Parks and Recreation,* or a TV show that's very formulaic; something that involves solving a case or a crime like *Law & Order* or *The Good Wife.*

For me, watching a show like *Parks and Rec* feels like coming home. I enter the world of Pawnee like I'm back at my family home for the holidays. I know the place well, I know the characters and their stories. I know which jokes make me cry from laughing and I know which episodes to skip because the plot line isn't as great as the others. There's also not a risk that I'll overdose. There won't be any new *Parks and Rec*, there's no direct impulse to get to the end. When I do, I can just start all over again, no big deal.

With the second type of shows, the *Law & Orders* of the world, I'm comforted by the fact that *most* cases are solved and things tend to be wrapped up quite neatly. The show isn't exactly 'light-hearted viewing' – it gets a lot of its inspiration from real-life tragedies happening in crime-riddled cities across America – but *Law & Order* has a narrative structure you can rely on. It's easily digestible.

The other thing is that shows like *Law & Order*, *Criminal Minds*, *Firefly* or even *The Simpsons* are episodic, which means they're self-contained. Every time you nestle in to watch an episode you're welcomed with conflict and resolution. You can also jump in at any point and jump around seasons and you can fall back into it wherever you want. There are also a LOT of episodes of *Law & Order*, which makes me feel calm. I don't have the pressure of HAVING to finish an entire season in one weekend because there are still loads to go. My brain likes the shows, it likes skipping from one problem to the next without having to solve it myself. There are amazing detectives to do that stuff.

From trying to keep track of all the things that make me feel good – dogs, TV shows, games – I've realised how much all of the little things make me feel alive and how much I want to stay alive, despite everything. Even in my darkest moments, on the end of the Tube platform or with a razor blade to my wrist, I have a well inside me that's all about life. I want to taste and feel and touch things. I want to be remembered. I want to help other people and I really want to be able to help myself. There's no way I can look at all the effort I've put into getting better and think, 'Wow, what a slacker.' I've done a lot and I will keep doing a lot and I'm proud of how committed and dedicated I am to my own aliveness.

I know that underneath all my issues there's a person who loves living. She likes zip wires and sharks and wild swimming and the first time a baby laughs. I try to activate that part as much as I can, even though it's especially hard when depression hits me like a ton of bricks and the 'alive' part of me lies dormant until the storm passes. Feeling alive to me largely means enjoying something new. Something that involves challenging my brain or challenging my body. Newness makes me feel refreshed, learning a new skill makes me feel proud. Even when I try something and immediately fail at it (e.g. the time I took an acrobatics class), I go home remembering how much fun I had.

Some other things that make me feel more alive:

- Liquorice that's so salty you have to suck on your tongue afterwards

Maggy van Eijk

- Having a warm shower and walking around the house butt naked afterwards
- Painting my toenails a neon colour
- Reading a poem that's so good it crashes straight into my skull
- Writing my own poem that's definitely not as good but it doesn't matter
- Lying flat on the floor listening to Radiohead in the dark
- Jumping in an ice-cold pond
- Lasting longer than I usually do in that ice-cold pond
- Doing a shoulder stand
- Doing a shoulder stand and not toppling over
- Going for a walk first thing in the morning
- Taking a train to a new city, getting out of the station and having no idea what to expect from my surroundings
- Photographing my friends in the woods when the sun is setting
- Swimming with friends where the exercise is actually coming from all the laughter rather than the swimming
- Cycling slowly in the rain
- Cycling fast through empty streets at midnight
- Cycling fast and singing 'Creep' at the top of my lungs

REMEMBER THIS WHEN YOU'RE SAD

- Having an incredible orgasm and lying there afterwards until it slowly subsides and everything feels easy
- Going to a gig and daring myself to inch closer to the front with every song
- Running into the sea in one go rather than dipping my toes in one by one
- Cooking a three-course meal for someone
- Seeing a work of art that makes me stand and stare until my back hurts
- That initial rushing feeling of walking into a roaringly packed football stadium
- Joining a march or a protest
- Making up a song from scratch, preferably in the shower
- Disembarking a rollercoaster and not quite believing I just survived that triple corkscrew
- Spotting family waiting for me at the arrivals gate of an airport
- Going to see a play that makes me cry
- Hugging a dog I haven't met before
- Hugging a dog I have met before
- Hugging a dog, any dog, every dog

15

REMEMBER THiS
WhEN YOU'RE SaD

Big girls don't cry; they fucking howl, wail, sob, yowl, pour buckets of tears out into the streets until there's a flood.

I cry all the time, and not just because of my mental health issues. In fact, my depression rarely makes me cry. Depression yanks the visceral emotions out of me and replaces them with a cold mist that haunts the corridors of my body. I cry because I'm sensitive, because things get to me easily and because sometimes I enjoy sitting in the bathtub with just a puddle of water and crying my fucking heart out. Some people love walking around naked or furiously wanking. I love having a cry.

Thanks to Facebook I cry daily. People love sharing

emotional videos about people overcoming incredible feats. I've spent a lot of my career making some of those videos, I know exactly how they work, what's going to get to people, and yet I'm not immune. There's a strand of emotional videos that always gets to me. It's not old people – I don't cry when I see cute grandpas (sorry) – it's the ones where dads do nice things for their kids.

I know it shouldn't be that magical, a dad doing a nice thing for their child, mums do nice things for their kids all the time and they don't have twenty-something women crying about it at their desk. Whatever, I'm only human. There's a video where a dad gives his toddler daughter a motivational speech in the mirror and soon enough my keyboard is drenched in all the salt water that has leaked out of my eyes.

I cry offline too. Just as easily. I once cried because I kicked a pebble onto the road and a car ran over it and I told myself I was a mass-murdering pebblist. I also cry when things don't go my way: when I leave my bank card at home, when I go to my friend's house to stay the night and forget to pack my meds or when someone shoves me on the escalator.

Sometimes my reasons for crying aren't especially good ones (the pebble for example), but the second I feel my eyes well up there's absolutely nothing I can do to stop the tear train. In the summer I enjoy the perk of wearing XXL shades to hide my outpourings of sadness.

In the winter it's trickier, but you can often blame it on a sharp wind.

I'm so dedicated to the crying cause I started jotting down all the places in public that let me have a good, satisfying weep. These places are useful either for being discreet, comfortable or a perfect match to my miserable mood. See if any of them work for you:

- At the front of the bus on the top level
- In a Bikram Yoga class
- In the back of an Uber
- In the self-help section of your favourite bookshop
- Alone in a rowing boat in a romantic park
- In a modern art museum
- In the queue for the post office
- In the queue for airport security
- In the queue for the night bus
- In an empty cinema
- In a McDonald's ballpit

- In your shower
- In your gym's shower
- In any goddamn shower
- By a self-checkout machine
- On top of a clock tower
- By the big copy machine at your work
- By the ready-made meals in your local supermarket
- On a rollercoaster
- On a water slide
- At a dog show
- In a garden centre where you can blame your allergies
- In the bridal section of a department store
- On a pier
- During a massage
- In the back of a bar under a table
- At the hairdresser after they show you what your new hair looks like
- In IKEA – anywhere will do, but bonus points if you can make it to the warehouse bit at the end where everyone is so exhausted you won't be the only one crying

The reason I'm banging on about crying is that I don't see anything wrong with it. I'm an emotional wreck most days. I can go from feeling like I'm owning everything to, in the next minute, despairing that my life is shit and nothing good will ever happen. It's very likely I'm going to be able to manage my emotions even better than I do now, but it's less likely I'm going to change fully. I'm always going to be what some have said is 'a bit much', 'a bit intense'. People have called me 'crazy', 'unstable', 'destructive', 'a burden', 'irresponsible' and, the gem, someone once said, 'You are going to die alone.'

Well, maybe I might but I'm going to make the absolute best of it until I do. I'm going to be as alive as I possibly can be. I'm going to take risks and take care of myself and the people I love and, when it feels safe, every so often, I'm going to let go and fall back into the world and see what the world has to offer me.

When I was fourteen years old, before a lot of the disordered eating and self-harm started, I'd just come back from prom at a school I'd just joined. We were living in Doha in Qatar in a compound filled with Range Rovers and maids and private pools. It was a strange world and it wouldn't be my world for long. A friend had dropped me off and before I decided to go into my house and say hi to my parents I went to the compound's public pool.

I was still wearing my prom dress, it was orange with a black band around the waist. I felt pretty, maybe even a bit glamorous. I liked the dress on me. I'd been flirting with a blonde-haired boy called Max I fancied. I'd been one of the first people to dance and I just felt really exhilarated about the whole evening. No one was at the pool, it was late and the darkness cloaked around the place like a dome.

I walked to the edge of the pool and turned round. My brain was clinging on to the last song I'd danced to: 'Baby If You Give It to Me' by Busta Rhymes and Mariah Carey. I hummed the song to myself until I let the lyrics go, like I was blowing a dandelion into the wind. I closed my eyes, took a deep breath and let myself fall backwards into the lukewarm water. I floated around on my back looking at the sky like it was the roof of my house. When I grew tired I climbed out and took my dress off and wrapped myself in a rogue towel that had been left behind by someone and walked back to my house smiling at my little adventure.

For me, that feeling by the swimming pool is something I remember when things are rough: a feeling of exuberant abandonment, of letting go and being just that little bit proud of myself. Some people wish to return to the safety of the womb, I want to return to the safety of that night. When I was young and ridiculous and filled with optimism.

When I'm sad – not weepy but properly fucking miserable – I remember how lucky I am I still have so many pools to fall backwards into. I have new journeys to make and stories to tell. I can't rewrite my past but I can use it as a guide for my future. I have an infinite amount of books to read and music to discover. I can get lost in the beauty of small things: a line in someone's brow, a dimple, a postcard, an orange peel, a jar of pencil shavings – there is so much I haven't encountered yet. There are so many breaths that are waiting to be taken away. I have loved and I'm able to love and I'll keep learning how to love even better than I do now.

The future is exciting, but the present can be just as thrilling if only I let it. Life is full of change and so am I. I can alter my perspective, my behaviour. I can regenerate. I can improve. I can work hard. I am brave, sometimes I am strong, and I'm grateful for both of those qualities. I've been through things I never thought I'd overcome.

So remember this: life is fucking hard sometimes but if you just keep going, just like you kept turning the pages of this book, you'll be OK.

16

REMEMBER THiS WHEN YOU'RE PREGNANT

When this book was released, I held a little 'OH MY GOD I DID IT' party in a cosy pub in south London. Friends showed up, my family were there and my grandparents made a surprise appearance from Holland. There was poetry, music and so much wine the pub actually ran out of glasses (shout out to everyone who provided me with pints of Pinot Grigio).

I was nervous and overwhelmed and so incredibly grateful that all these people were in one room celebrating something I'd created. I ended the night in my local kebab shop with my boyfriend Alex and my friend Rik and I had this sneaky feeling that that moment, halloumi wrap and soggy chips and all, would be one of the best moments in my whole life.

Little did I know that somewhere buried deep inside my belly, past all the nerves and alcohol and fried halloumi, lay a teeny tiny foetus.

I wouldn't find out about this foetus until a month later. I did a pregnancy test in my work loo because my boobs were getting abnormally large. I'd joked that all the iced buns I was eating were going straight to my breasts, but after making that joke a few too many times I thought it was time to pee on a stick.

I bought a test at Boots and walked to the toilets. The BBC is a pretty impressive place – you can't help but feel a little chill when you walk into New Broadcasting House and gaze across the buzzing newsroom. However, the one annoying thing about the building (next to a distinct lack of mugs) is that there aren't enough toilets to go around. When I did finally get a free cubicle, I felt anxious about holding everyone else up. I was going to be in there for a good while. I took a deep breath, muttered an apology under my breath to the people waiting for me and peed on the stick. It was going to be negative anyway. I was on the pill and my boobs were just having a 'moment'. It's fine. No big deal.

I peeked at the urine-soaked device (I can never get the midstream motion right). I didn't have to wait for the results, I'd bought a fancy one so it even told me the amount of weeks straightaway. I looked at it and thought: 'LOL'. I couldn't really formulate another thought.

I was on a time constraint too. Aside from all the other ladies who needed to pee, I had to pick up my freelancer friend who was waiting for me in reception. (Funnily enough it was the talented illustrator Flo who did the illustrations in this book.)

I walked towards the lift like a robot trying its damn hardest not to break down. My upper lip was sweaty, my vision was pixelated but I focused on taking one footstep at a time. I inhaled deeply and tried not to get the urine-covered stick out of my pocket and tell everyone in the lift that shit was about to go down.

I picked up Flo and walked her to her desk, but before she even settled into her seat I blurted out: 'This is a lot of information to take in so don't freak out, but I just did a pregnancy test and it said "pregnant".'

Flo, who is truly a pragmatic unicorn, tinkered with my brain and set it on a very handy autopilot mode. It told me to return to Boots, get at least four more tests, take them into the loo and see what they each had to say before forming a reaction.

Before I knew it, I was back in one of the cubicles, this time unfortunately tainted by a horrific smell unleashed from someone's bowels. Skid marks stared back at me like angry caterpillars. 'Great,' I thought. 'I'm going to find out I'm pregnant in a shit-stained work loo breathing in someone else's poo fumes.' Well, that's exactly how I found out. All the tests were positive. I was 100 per cent pregnant.

My initial reaction was a subdued 'Yes!' but wrapped in a lot of 'Holy fuck'. I'm not going to lie: this pregnancy was entirely unplanned. Sorry baby if you're reading this, all the best things in life are unplanned, so don't worry. (Apart from STDs and surprise birthday parties, of course.)

As I began to process everything over the next weeks a part of me felt that the responsible decision would be to terminate the pregnancy. I'd just written a book detailing the ins and outs of my mental instability, my Twitter feed is a shriek-y cesspit of oversharing which doesn't exactly scream 'has it together' and financially I'd only just settled into a new job – I was still living from one pay cheque to the next. I did have an *amazing* boyfriend, but we'd been together for less than a year and we didn't live together. Where was our baby going to sleep?

Despite all of these things, there was something in me that really, really wanted this baby. I remember telling my therapist that I felt like I'd spent my whole life trying to find a reason not just to stay alive, but to look after myself. I could never do it for me. I could do it for my family, a boyfriend, but eventually the self-destruction would lure me away from a healthy life and I'd hurt myself again, either emotionally or physically.

After each falling down I tried so hard to get it together, to follow a self-care plan, to get back into swimming and eating properly instead of inhaling £5 corner shop wine every night. I'd fuck up relationships, friendships and jobs all because I ultimately never learnt how to care about me. If I was my own child I was only just about keeping myself alive. However, having someone else to dedicate every inch of energy, love and compassion to meant that I could do this properly. Maybe I could finally get my life together.

Unfortunately, no matter how much you want your life together, willpower isn't going to do it alone. The financial and emotional stress was like a constant hammering against my temples. When people congratulated me on my pregnancy I just wanted to whisper, 'But you don't know, you don't know how hard it's going to be. I might be totally shit at this.' So I'd shrug and change the topic.

As I'm writing this I'm well into my second trimester. When I told my boyfriend he was incredibly excited, and I have no doubt he's going to be a wonderful father. He's pretty much a dad to me already so having another unruly person running around the flat won't be too much of a shock. I've told everyone else close to me and I've even posted a picture of my leaking breasts on Instagram. It's official: I'm definitely having this child.

Even after I passed through the often hellish first trimester and made it out of the miscarriage danger zone, my pregnancy anxiety didn't subside much. I found that just as I trained my brain to stop worrying about one thing another fear, symptom or dread would pop up.

On top of all the little things I stress about there's the big overarching worry that buzzes over my head like a neon sign: I WON'T BE A GOOD MUM. I often find myself crafting a mental list of all the reasons I'm in no way fit for motherhood. Some examples:

- I can't tie my shoelaces (I just kind of bunch them together and hope for the best)
- I can only tell the difference between left and right by guesswork and a leap of faith
- I can't drive; most mums seem to know how to drive
- I don't care a great deal about personal hygiene if I'm really honest
- If my organs wouldn't fail I'd eat crisps all the time
- I do pretty much just eat crisps all the time
- I do have a great boyfriend and partner in crime but as much as I love the guy he has never, ever read a single Harry Potter book and this is very stressful to me
- My attention span lasts about a minute
- My favourite type of humour involves farts
- I never do my tax returns on time, and in fact I still don't fully understand what tax returns actually are
- No plant has ever made it past two days in my care

This is a very small version of the list; it spans pages and pages and I add to it on a daily basis. Thanks to years of therapy, I know that lists like this are incredibly damaging and can cause your mind to spin out of control. So when I sense this happening, I try to recall a counter-list. Just a few key statements that contradict the UNFIT MOTHER siren that goes off in my head:

- Whilst I love calling myself dumb, ditzy and stupid (like a trio of Disney mice), I do have some semblance of emotional intelligence. I can always tell when someone is upset. I've spotted people about to burst into tears across the office. I have a sixth sense for sadness and I don't just let other people's distress slide. I do genuinely care about people and I want to make their situation better. So perhaps there will be times with my child when I care too much and they'll roll their eyes and slam their door on me but I know I'll never, ever give up

- I have a good imagination. Whenever I've babysat or nannied for small children I've spent hours building forts out of bedsheets and chairs or pretending the living room was actually space and we're all astronauts fighting aliens in zero gravity conditions. I've invented games out of sticks and bits of paper. I once ran an afterschool club with

no resources and we competed in an imaginary
Olympics just jumping over hurdles made from
air. Maybe one day I'll be rich (I'll learn to make
hipster jam and sell it at farmers' markets),
but for the next few years I imagine my kid's
favourite toys will be a spatula and a puppet made
from socks, but we'll make the most of it. I know
I'll always put effort in: there will be memory
boxes and activity jars and walls of drawings
and handprints. My kid, if nothing else, will have
creativity, music and laughter

● Whilst I'm not the most maternal person in the
world, I know I will do absolutely all I can to
protect my kid, to make sure nothing bad happens
to them. I'll teach them all the things I've learnt
– some of the things they can read in this book,
although they'll be way too busy reading *War and
Peace* in Russian to care about their mum's mental
health memoir

● I know I haven't always kept myself safe or really
looked after myself, but what I've never been
quite able to do for me, I know I'll do it for the
little person who came out of me. They can join
me in my cold-water swimming, happy crying to
Lorde and eating salty liquorice until our gums
ache. All of the things that make me incredibly
happy I can pass onto them. (But, real talk for a

second, if they don't consider *Melodrama* to be
one of the best albums ever made I'm stuffing
them back up my cervix)

I've had to try hard to let go of this 'good mum'
construct I've conjured up in my head. A construct
someone like me could never fit. If I had to draw my
perfect mum I'd give her skinny jeans, because of course
she got her body back into shape in no time; a white and
black stripy T-shirt (I live in south London – this is pretty
much mum uniform); Converse shoes; hair swept up in
a tidy ponytail (not the raggedy end of the broomstick
you'll often see on my head); a pram that costs as much as
my rent; a coffee on the go; a baby that's happy and smiley
and alert. She's someone who can take a work call and
breastfeed at the same time. She goes jogging and takes
the baby with her. She volunteers in the charity shop and
pops the baby in a sling. The baby eats organic food, is
super healthy but enjoys the occasional brioche bun. She
probably runs a start-up and a successful blog and has an
Instagram account that makes money and gets her lots of
free stuff without being overtly full of self-promotion.

There are billions of mums around the world. If they
all looked like the ones in my head we'd live in some kind
of hipster *Stepford Wives* hell. A good mum can look however the hell she wants, and yes, maybe even I can look
like a good mum. Just because you don't fit into the ideal

of whatever you or society has built around parenthood doesn't mean you're not right. These projections are fantasy billboards that follow us around and make us feel shit. They exist in body image and career prospects and beauty and sexuality and the list goes on forever. Motherhood isn't free from them unfortunately. Ignore the billboards towering over you. Tear them down, smash them, kick them and take a big dump on them if that helps.

If you've got this far you'll know this book has been all about my experience with mental health conditions. Well, when you're pregnant your mental health gets a little kick up the backside. On top of the fact that your brain is a slow cooker filled with hormones just stewing away, all your before-pregnancy mental health conditions are still there. They haven't taken a back seat to let you focus on your big life change. Nope, they're still bubbling away.

First step is to make sure your GP and/or midwife is made aware of your mental health conditions. Once you've done this you'll most likely be offered additional support on top of the regular antenatal appointments. What you're offered will largely depend on where you live and the resources available in your area. I was assigned to a team of midwives who have experience with mums-to-be with mental health conditions. I was also offered an appointment with an NHS counsellor to talk about an action plan for looking after my mental health leading up to birth and afterwards.

I was offered additional meetings with the NHS counsellor and her wider team to make sure I'm doing OK. This includes increased visits after the birth in case I develop post-partum depression. I also check in more regularly with my GP about my medication. I was initially told I should come off my SSRIs completely, but just dropping down one dosage caused a bit of a brain blip. Depression seeped into my head shrouding everything in fog. I was already tired because of the whole being pregnant thing but I'd sit on the floor in my work loos and stare into the white wall until I'd forget where I was. When I'd get home I'd go straight to bed but not before I'd cry about how I was going to be a terrible parent and that no one was going to help me because I didn't deserve any help.

When I'd balanced out a little the thought of dropping back down a dosage terrified me. Instead, I stayed on all my medication, despite there being some small risks. There's a lot of shame – both internally and societally – around taking medication during pregnancy. However, both my midwife and I decided it was more important to keep my mental health in balance, especially with my life being turned upside down. Now just wasn't the time to ditch the thing that had helped clear the fog for me for all those years. There'd be another time for that.

Body confidence in pregnancy was also a weird one for me because it's suddenly considered very normal for people you barely know to comment on your body, like it's been put on stage. As I write this, my bump is still relatively small, so a lot of comments are along the lines of: 'Oh you don't look pregnant at all, your belly is so tiny!' I don't find this offensive but it makes me feel incredibly insecure because in my head 'you don't look pregnant' can easily be translated to 'you don't look like a REAL mum! YOU WILL BE A SHIT MUM!'. I'm enjoying all the changes my body is going through; I find it fascinating, even the gross and slightly weird stuff. I just don't want other people paying attention to it. It's my body after all.

Another thing I've been finding difficult in pregnancy is dissociation. If I had my way I'd be totally present during the entire nine months and beyond. I want to be aware of all the ways my body grows to accommodate another person like a house. I want to notice all the kicks, bumps, flutters and stretches. I want to write it all down, ask questions and respond to questions and just be totally here for all of it. However, there have been times where despite wanting to be immersed in the experience my mind retreated: I was there but I wasn't really there. Most frustratingly this happened during the 20-week scan, called the anomaly scan, where they check for any abnormalities.

I'm nothing but grateful for the care I've received but any appointment or scan will at the very least involve your blood being taken and peeing in a cup, so your initial 'yay I'm going to see my baby' excitement is slightly dampened by feeling like a lab rat.

Scans are an incredible feat of science and technology. I've also been lucky that my baby hasn't had any severe abnormalities show up so far, but despite that, the process of getting a scan done felt pretty strange. You lie there, feeling a bit clueless about what they're about to show you. Various faces hover over you and hands and instruments push down on your belly. Sometimes multiple people push your belly at once. In front of you is a big TV screen and it's hard to believe what you're seeing up there is actually inside of you. I felt like I should go 'aw' when the doctor said 'Look, there's the leg!' but all I could think was 'FUCKING HELL THERE'S A HUMAN LEG WEDGED INSIDE ME RIGHT NOW'.

The surrealness of the scan took a darker turn for me due to elements of my past that bubbled up to my brain's surface. When you've experienced trauma, particularly sexual trauma, there may be times when the memory of what happened creeps back into you like hot, thick tar. Whilst the scans are conducted in safe environments, I still felt exposed and vulnerable. Lying down, seeing those heads hovering over me, I immediately felt transported

273

back to waking up in a bed I didn't recognise, seeing a man having sex with my body without my consent.

I couldn't quite explain to anyone what was happening during the scan. The hot blur in my eyes worked its way up into a sting. I hoped everyone in the room thought my eyes were watering at the sight of my healthy baby, when actually I wanted to run out of the room. I tried to distract myself by making jokes about our baby having my egg-shaped head. Between taking pictures of the scan my boyfriend held my hand and I focused on the warm feeling of his skin on mine. I tried to bring myself back into the present by clenching and unclenching my toes over and over but nothing worked. The tar had separated my mind into fragmented chunks. Even though I was told my baby was 'perfect', nothing about the situation felt perfect at all.

After the scan my boyfriend returned to work and I got in the bath and cried for about five hours. I was incredibly scared. I was scared for my baby, and of all of the things that could happen to them that I can't protect them from. I was scared that I wouldn't be present for any of the scans to come or the birth or any of the moments after. I was scared that I'd look at my baby after labour and think 'meh' and not connect with them at all.

When I spoke with the NHS counsellor I mentioned the dissociation and how the scan took me back to my sexual assault. I waited for her to look at me with a worried, disapproving expression. Instead, she assured me that this was quite common for survivors, and that notes could be added to my file to ensure I feel as safe as possible going forward. I could choose to have fewer internal exams or just get more of a warning when they are about to happen. As long as I'm not in an emergency situation I can request to have no male staff present, if possible. I hadn't known about these options and I'm incredibly relieved I decided to voice my fears despite the shame I felt.

As this goes to print, I'll be in my final month of pregnancy and, who knows, I might even have a baby by then (please send treats). Once that tiny little human learns to read and decides to humour their mum and pick this book up, I hope they remember some of the things in this book. If you're reading this, little human, I've added in one final list for you. Here we go:

- Don't rush your way through life, because the difficult parts won't last forever and the really great parts are over before you know it
- Bad things always seem to happen all at once. It's not your fault. It's just how life challenges you
- You can take it one day at a time, but taking it one hour at a time is fine too
- Find absolute joy in the little things and never feel ashamed of what they are, whether it's running

over freshly cut grass, eating heaps of icing sugar or spending 11 hours on The Sims

- You don't have to find your 'one thing' to be good at, you can be semi-decent at lots of different things. It makes life more fun

- Learn to trust people. Even if you've been let down or hurt most people are ultimately very good, you just have to let them in. Try not to expect the worst all the time

- Praise other people in your life as much as you possibly can. Treat your friends well, big them up and leave a thousand hearts on all their selfies

- Always take time to talk to the quietest people in the room; they're the most interesting

- If you're at a party and there's a dog, literally ditch all of the people (including the quiet person, sorry). The dog should be your only focus

- Remember that your mum is a little bit insane and will probably make you feel embarrassed all the time, but she loves you more than anything in this whole entire world

Acknowledgements

A couple years ago Laura Williams approached me about becoming my agent and my first reaction was "WHYHHHYYYYYYYY!?!" until I stopped nervous screaming and said yes. This pretty much sums up our relationship. Laura tells me about a great opportunity, I stare at her in terror and she convinces me that I should go for it and it's a good thing. Thanks to Laura's support as an agent and friend I was able to complete this book without dying from anxiety in the process. Also thanks to everyone else at PFD, especially Marilia who has been nothing but supportive and enthusiastic and is an absolute babe.

Thank you to everyone at Bonnier: Natalie, Ellis, September and the eagle-eyed copy editors. Thank you to

Morwenna who sent me a lovely email after reading my first draft when I was feeling very "ugh this book is dumb". It really put the spark back into my brain. Thank you.

Sladjana over at Unieboek | Het Spectrum AKA the boss queen of the Dutch publishing industry – thank you!!! Sladjana has been a champion of my ideas and my very existence since the day we met. Thank you for making me feel like a rock star every time I'm with you.

Special thanks to all the comrades I met at BuzzFeed. When my brain decided to do a nosedive into hell there were some fantastic people who dug me out of despair. I can't thank you enough. I love you Kim, Kelly, Francis, Laura G, Remee (for realising things), Gena (for speaking things into existence), Hannah (for paving the way with your iconic book and badassery). Big love to Victoria for trusting me and being a fellow anxious bee. Thank you to everyone in the union chat group. Thank you to all of you who sent kind messages and had my back. I will never, ever forget. Thank you Paul Hamilos for taking me out to that Korean place and telling me in the kindest way possible to get my shit together. Thank you for telling me about your own mental health. Thank you for making me feel less alone. Thank you Dan. Sorry you had to be there in my ugliest hour. Thank you for literally picking me up. Thank you for not letting go.

Thanks to everyone I've ever spoken to online about mental health: on Instagram, Twitter, Facebook groups, Reddit and in the comments of some of my BuzzFeed posts. Thank you for making me feel like I was doing something important. Thank you to my therapist Susannah who has given me a handle on my life. Thanks for teaching me how to be less of a dick to myself.

Thank you to new friends I've made at the BBC. Thanks Megha for letting me vent and thanks for never judging. Thanks to the very cool team at BBC Studios Digital. Thanks for being supportive about my book. Thanks for letting me work on the 1 in 4 campaign. It meant so much to be part of it.

Thanks to wonderful Flo who elevated this book with her illustrations. Thank you for being so excited about this project from the start. Thanks for going on this trip with me. Thanks for laughing at all my jokes even when they're fucking weird. Thanks for making me feel good about myself. You're one of a kind. I love you dearly.

Thank you to my amazing friend Laura Brouwer who is so talented and beautiful and intelligent and beautiful and kind and beautiful (yes I'm totally in love with you). Thank you for always being proud of me. You are my family. Thank you Vi, the crazy French lady. You always know what to say, and you always always have my back. Thank you Ilayda who taught me so many things it's ridiculous. Thanks for always being there when I need help with my vagina and my brain. Thanks for introducing me to the BPD reddit thread when I was desperate for people who'd understand. Thanks for being unashamedly honest and brave. You're a fucking icon. Hannah, my human golden retriever. Thank you for your long rambling texts that would give Tolstoy a run for his money. Thank you for being so caring and a dedicated cheerleader even when I've properly screwed my life up, you make me feel like it's not that bad, it's fine, it's SO FINE! I love you and your brain and your bravery so much and I will never stop loving all of the things about you.

Thank you to my fantastic family. Mum, Dad, Rein, Sandy, Annie & Tim. I know it's not easy reading a lot of this stuff and thank you for sticking by me and lifting me up. Sandy you're a dreamboat of a little brother. I love you. You're so bloody wise – how are you only 12 years old (kidding!). Annie you will always be my favourite role model. You are the most incredible woman. I'm lucky to be related to you. Thank you to Alex's parents: Chris and Pat. Thank you for saying such lovely things about my writing. Thank you Jay AKA Amaroun you're so unbelievably talented and kind to me! Thanks to Cord and Rik who let me do a lot of writing in their house and use their hot water. Thank you Rik for giving me the idea of a book launch and I guess you can come if you want, whatever, ugh.

And lastly to my boyfriend Alex: thanks for everything. Ok, bye!!

LOL. Alex. Goddamnit. There's too much to say. You're so handsome it's too much. Thanks for being a sounding board for every thought that enters my head. Thanks for being totally chill and supportive when I asked you to read my first draft. Let's face it a lot of this book talks about other dudes I boned, which isn't fun to read. Thanks for being so filled with kindness and love and being so generous with that love. Thanks for being patient, especially with my BPD, which is kind of like dating a woman with a poisonous sea urchin for a heart. I know the main way I show you I love you is by wrestling you to the ground or prodding your belly button or shouting inappropriate things in public places but jokes aside: I'm completely overwhelmed by how much you changed my life for the better. You made me realise I can be more than someone's "crazy ex-girlfriend" I can be someone's crazy current girlfriend and sometimes I can even be just a girlfriend full stop.

And lastly to everyone who has found themselves in the pages of this book. You're not broken. You're not losing it. Keep going. Take baby steps. Be kind to yourself and don't forget to go out there and pet as many dogs as you can.